Life Lessons from the Heart

Life Lessons from the Heart

Twelve Strategies for Achieving Personal Success and Fulfilment

---

Dr. H. S. Broderick-Scott

iUniverse LLC
Bloomington

LIFE LESSONS FROM THE HEART
TWELVE STRATEGIES FOR ACHIEVING PERSONAL SUCCESS
AND FULFILMENT

Unless otherwise indicated, scriptures are taken from the Holy Bible, Red Letter Edition, containing the Old and New Testaments in the King James Version. Copyright ©1984, 1977 by Thomas Nelson, Inc.

This book is written for adults who are interested in a step-by-step guide to success. In everything you do, you'll need to have a plan.

iUniverse books may be ordered through booksellers or by contacting:

iUniverse LLC
1663 Liberty Drive
Bloomington, IN 47403
www.iuniverse.com
1-800-Authors (1-800-288-4677)

ISBN: 978-1-4917-1764-6 (sc)
ISBN: 978-1-4917-1766-0 (hc)
ISBN: 978-1-4917-1765-3 (e)

Printed in the United States of America.

iUniverse rev. date: 01/20/2014

Contents

Acknowledgements

I would like to extend a sincere thank-you to my family for supporting me and my love of service throughout the years. Thank you for sharing me with others as I developed the mentoring programme. You have been a tower of strength, and I will always love you unconditionally.

I'm incredibly grateful to my talented daughters, Nikka and Shay-Ann, for their help, support, and words of encouragement. I am especially thankful for my gifted daughter Nikka, who reviews and edits all of my work and who helps to keep me focused. I hope that one day she will realize just how talented she is.

Special thanks to all the young men and women with whom I've had the pleasure to serve as mentor over the years. The relationships we've developed have been very special. The fact that I've had the opportunity to get to know so many of you and play a small role in your lives means the world to me. These relationships inspired me to write this book!

To Mrs. Virginia Plowright, a teacher at Clarendon College in Jamaica as well as the coordinator for the mentoring and scholarship programmes: thanks for your words of encouragement. Our conversations about the students made me realize that writing this book could be a blessing to others.

Finally, I'd like to thank two of my teachers. To my former English teacher at Clarendon College, Mrs. Pansie Porteous, whose winsome personality and brilliant mind have been an inspiration to many of her students. And to Mrs. Catherine Jones, who had the uncanny ability to bring out the best in us during her commercial and typing classes. Thanks for sharing your gifts with us and for impacting my life through your teachings.

Introduction

Nothing in life has any meaning except the meaning you give it.

—Anthony Robbins

When I was growing up, there were two things I knew I wanted in life. I wanted to have children, and I wanted to teach. I am happy to say that I have been able to accomplish both of these things. I have three beautiful daughters and seven wonderful grandchildren; they fill my heart with so much joy that words alone cannot explain. My daughters have grown from babies into little girls, and from little girls into grown women who now tell *me* what do, what to eat, how to dress, how to dance, and even what music to listen to! I often protest, but truthfully I appreciate their input because it keeps me young!

I wasn't a very demanding parent; I didn't force my dreams on them. When it came time to choose a career, I allowed my children to have their own dreams and do the things that made them happy. It was always my hope that they would be safe, loving, kind, respectful, and well educated. But most of all, I wanted them to find a way to unlock their full potential and be the best they could, fulfilling their goals and purposes in life with honesty and integrity. I've done my best to instil in them the values my parents taught me. I taught them to love and care for others knowing that God would allow the blessings to flow back to them and their families. When I was a child, my mother would always encourage us to treat others the way we would like to be treated, thereby instilling in us the fact that kindness is the greatest gift of all.

When I was growing up in Jamaica, I noticed the way my mother and stepfather would reach out to help people in the community, and it made me want to do the same. Children often came to my home with the hope of learning to read and write. I taught them as we sat together on the veranda on weekends. My friends also came over to study in the afternoons, and we completed various homework assignments together. Many of these children did not have their own textbooks, and working together gave us all a chance to do well. My mother was one of the kindest women I knew, because at home there were always children from the neighbourhood, and at dinnertime every one of them was fed. She had a special gift of making something out of nothing, and she never refused a hungry child because there wasn't enough. She always made sure there was food for everyone. I believe this was her way of teaching us to be kind to others and showing us that being able to share is a gift from God.

Developing a mentoring programme was my way of caring for children who are in need. Not only do these children need a good education, but they also need guidance, food, and clothing. Most important of all, they need to know that there are people who believe in them and truly care for them. My intention in creating the mentoring programme was very clear from the beginning: I wanted to create a programme through which I would have the opportunity to do the following:

- help to connect present and future generations by bringing people together
- encourage mentors to work closely with their mentees, listen to them, guide them, and become sources of inspiration. But most of all, they should serve as positive role models.

This programme allows us as mentors to experience that realization every day through the letters and emails from students who express their gratitude for the programme and the people in their lives. I am ever so thankful for the many mentors who contribute their time, money, and services to help make these children's dreams of achieving their educational goals a reality. I will always be grateful to my mentors who were there for me when I needed someone to listen to, help make things less complicated, and help me make the right choices. I appreciate all they have done to make me realize that in giving back, I, too, can help make a difference.

Over the years I have taught and served as a mentor to students from various countries and very diverse cultural backgrounds. I have also developed a special relationship with these young men and women. Some have gone on to become doctors, researchers, journalists, nurses, lawyers, engineers, soldiers, and teachers; others are still in school and aspiring towards their future careers. I am very proud of them. I believe in them and truly love them. The fact that they have allowed me to play a small role in their lives has helped to make me a better person. One of the most important truths I've learned serving as a mentor is that people are always looking for someone to guide them, and for someone they can count on to teach them how to achieve success. *Life Lessons from the Heart* is written with the paramount idea of sharing some valuable life principles which I consider to be lessons of love. These twelve strategies will teach, among other things:

- how to have a clear vision and mission
- how to set goals and develop a plan of action
- how to develop good character, focusing on honesty, integrity, compassion, and courage
- how to develop good leadership skills
- how to be grateful in all aspects of your life
- how to build lasting and meaningful relationships, focusing on friendships, intimate relationships, relationships with your own children, and relationships with children and their peers
- how to manage your finances
- how to teach your children about money

- how to take care of yourself and your family, and how to manage the stress in your life
- how to nurture your spirituality
- how to be culturally sensitive
- how to become a mentor and be of service to others.

It is my hope that after reading these twelve life principles, readers will realize that nothing can stop them from achieving success in their lives if they have the right mental attitude. It is also my hope that parents will find it quite helpful in teaching their children how they can best fulfil their desires and successfully attain their goals. The examples I've chosen to illustrate these lessons have touched my heart and my spirit in a very personal way, and I've tried to put it all together as authentically as possible. I hope that these lessons and stories will awaken your spirit and cause you to feel a personal connection, because they were written straight from the heart.

As you continue on your personal journey through life, you will be faced with many obstacles. Some may seem impossible to overcome. However, know this: the favour of God will allow you to overcome all obstacles, and he will never give you more than you can handle. Making wise decisions, planning ahead of time, focusing on your goals, staying positive, and having faith will help to make the journey much easier. Think of it this way: when heading out on the road for a drive, you know there are three things you *must* have with you—your driver's license, proof of registration, and car insurance. However, you never know what can happen, so having some sort of roadside assistance and the phone number for a good mechanic can be a lifesaver in the event of an emergency. Likewise, if you own a home, you'll want to take preventative measures such as investing in a home-monitoring system and purchasing homeowner's insurance. Some may say that all of this is not necessary, but I believe that it is better to be prepared than to have to say in the end, "I wish I had done that."

I believe that the same manner in which you plan for your car and home is necessary for you to plan for your educational, personal, spiritual, and professional journey. As you navigate your way through the pages of this book and read these twelve life principles, I hope you will come to know yourself much better and that you will realize that you can be or do anything you want in life. These principles are designed to help make the journey much smoother and less complicated. Over the years these lessons have been very helpful to me, both personally and professionally. They are like tools you can use to achieve personal success and fulfilment in life. I hope you will value these lessons and share them with others. I understand that no two lives are the same, so you may have to tweak a few things to fit your own situation, but I can assure you that if you read these lessons of love with an open heart and apply some of the basic principles to your everyday life, the results can be amazing!

Having a clear vision simply means that you have a specific intent for the future; you know exactly what you want to do. Your mission is what you are doing daily to achieve this goal.

Lesson 1: Have a Clear Vision and a Mission

We all have dreams, and sometimes these dreams are much bigger than our faith. No matter what others might say, we can't allow them to distract us or talk us out of our dreams. If you believe in your dream and can imagine it coming to pass, then you can work to make it a reality. Having a clear vision means that you have created a mental map of what you would like to do, what you would like to be, or what you would like to see happen in the future. The images you create in your mind will help to determine your destination. Your imagination is so incredibly powerful, and so it is important to create positive images in your minds in order to have a positive outcome.

Each of us as human beings should want success and happiness in life. Just like any organization, in order for you to be successful, it is important for you to have a plan for your life, a clear vision. Your vision should be future-based, and it should be aligned with what you would truly like to accomplish. This plan will help you to set your essential goal and point you in the direction in which you wish to grow. The Bible clearly states in Proverbs 29:18, "Where there is no vision, the people perish." No matter what is going on in your life today, know that God has bigger and better things planned for your future. You have a purpose and a destiny to fulfil, so be hopeful, get excited, and take steps to make it happen.

As you pursue your dreams, don't be surprised if you are faced with fear. Sometimes it's simply fear of the unknown. You will find that the more important your dreams are, the bigger the fear becomes. Don't allow this fear to sabotage your ideas and cause you to abandon your dreams. Let go of those unwanted thoughts and those annoying voices in your head that are saying that you are not good enough, or that you are not capable of doing the work required to make your dream a reality. Take time to sit by yourself in a moment of silence and pray. When you pray, ask God to help you to overcome your fears, and as you sit in that silence, allow the spirit to lead you and guide your thoughts in a positive direction so that you will gain the strength and the courage to move forward. It is also important to understand that the greatest battle you will have in life is becoming who you would like to be, fulfilling your dreams, and achieving your goals in the face of adversity.

Sometimes you will find that your plans for the future are stalled because of what is going on around you. Don't allow your environment to prevent you from dreaming big dreams; think outside the box and do something bold, something different. Most of all, don't simply sit back and *hope* for things to happen. If you want your dreams to come true, you cannot continue sleeping—you have to wake up and make them happen. You have to move forward with confidence and work diligently towards achieving your goals. Many people wake up each day and pray for God to help them make their dreams a reality, but prayer without the work will not help one realize one's vision. I believe that prayer should be followed by action, because this is a demonstration of faith. If you do the work required, God will appreciate your hard work and provide the assistance you need along the way. Martin Luther King Jr. said, "Faith is taking the first step even when you don't get to see the whole staircase."

Be careful not to confuse your vision with your mission. Your vision is what helps to provide the focus you need. Having a clear vision simply means that you have a specific intent for the future, that you know exactly what you want to do. Your mission is what you are doing daily to achieve this goal. As you think about your vision, ask yourself this question: "Will I be able to convince others that my ideas and my plans will help to make a difference?" This is a very important question to consider. Whatever your plans are, you want to do something that will have an impact on the lives of others, something that will truly make a difference. In the process you'll want others to buy into your idea and come to the realization that what you are doing is important.

As you work through this process, there may be a few bumps along the way, but never give up. Always remain positive and know that if you take the time to think about it, and if you truly believe in yourself and your abilities, then there is nothing to prevent you from achieving your goal. If you need encouragement, speak with someone you trust, or do what I did and write it down. When I was preparing for my graduate degree, I used notecards and sticky notes to write words of encouragement, my goals and objectives, as well as the strategies I wanted to implement in order to accomplish these goals. I had them posted on my bedroom door, next to the mirror in my bathroom, by my computer, on the refrigerator, and on my front door. They were the last things I saw before leaving the house. It caused something to happen to me deep down inside, because I had something to look forward to, and it also served as a constant, daily, visual reminder of where I was heading. Many of my friends laughed at me, but others thought it was a good idea. You can do the same thing. Write your vision and your mission on a piece of paper. Leave copies in various places such as on the dashboard in your car and even somewhere on your desk at work or at home. Believe me when I say that you will find this to have a very powerful impact on the way you feel about your ideas and your plans.

Once you believe in what you've set out to do, have confidence in yourself and share your ideas with friends and family members you can trust. When they see how passionate you are and how hard you're working, they may become interested enough to offer assistance. As you move forward with your plans, there are a few important points to remember.

- Surround yourself with positive people who will encourage you.
- Remove or ignore anyone whose intentions are to sow seeds of doubt or negativity.
- Forget about what others have to say and their opinions about who you should be.
- Ignore the criticisms of others and don't allow them to become a distraction in your life. Instead, use this as motivation to move forward with your plans.
- Stand firm for what you believe in; know who you are, and feel good about your ideas.
- Work hard and stay on course, knowing that in all that you do, your success will be measured by the breadth of your vision and the depth of your convictions.

Each and every one of us has a purpose in life, but in order to realize what our true purposes are, we must first have dreams. This is where it all begins, and you have to focus on that dream, create your vision and your mission, and work towards making it a reality. When you have a clear vision and a mission for your life, you should be able to feel it burning deep within. This feeling should be so great that it empowers you to move forward. Imagine an artiste such as John Legend having a great idea about a song. He can't sleep, so he decides to sit at the piano and work this out. With every stroke of the keys on the piano, the song begins to come to life. But he doesn't stop there—he continues to work at it, making notes and making changes, until after hours of work, this beautiful song is completed. Before you know it time has passed, and his song becomes number one on the charts because the people love it and purchase his album. Later on he'll realize that he is being nominated for a Grammy Award. All of this happened because he had a vision and a mission, and he stuck to it, working hard to ensure that this was accomplished. Even though he is such a talented person, the good things in his life do not come easy—he has to work for it. Sometimes things don't work out the way he would like them to, but he doesn't give up, and he works at it until he is successful.

You, too, should follow your dreams and not allow others to distract you from fulfilling your purpose in life. You should be confident, maintain a positive outlook on whatever you are doing, and work diligently towards making your dream a reality. When you have big dreams, you can't expect that everything you want is going to happen overnight. You also have to expect that the challenges will be big. Therefore, it's important for you to prepare yourself for these challenges and find ways to deal with them as they come along. Just know that not everyone will like you, and some might even be jealous of your success. But whatever the situation might be, you can't spend time to sweat the small stuff; you have to stay focused. God has empowered you to do great and wonderful things with your dreams, so be confident and move forward in faith, and success will be well within your reach.

Success is about setting realistic goals and having the strength and conviction to move forward with tenacity and great determination.

Lesson 2: Set Goals and Develop a Plan of Action

People set goals because they want to be successful. In order to be successful, it is important to set goals that are realistic, measurable, and achievable before continuing on to more lofty ones. As you work towards achieving these goals, you will need to develop a strategic plan of action with realistic timelines; this will help you to pace yourself and stay focused. Successful people do these things and work diligently to see their dreams come to fruition. Whether you want to work in the business sector or become a doctor, teacher, athlete, actor, dancer, model, or fashion designer, you must set realistic and measurable goals.

The world is crying out for leaders whose goals are to build up, not to tear down, to nurture and not to exploit. Your goals reflect your vision for your life; they should have real meaning and show important aspects of your future success. Think of them as pit stops along your journey. Your plan of action is like a road map, a step-by-step guide to help you get to your destination. Achieving realistic goals will give you the confidence to raise the bar. As you do so, don't be afraid to dream big, because the only way you will fail is if you fail to try. Look at it this way: everything that exists started with a dream. As Napoleon Hill said, "Failure is a trickster with a keen sense of irony and cunning. It takes great delight in tripping one when success is almost within reach." If you believe in yourself, stay positive, and do the work required, then your dreams will ultimately become a reality.

As you begin to set your goals, here are a few important tips for you to consider.

- Set goals that are very clear and specific, with realistic time limits and steps for achieving them.
- Write your goals down on a piece of paper, on your computer, or even on a tablet. Writing them down helps to make them seem even more real, something tangible you can actually look forward to.
- Place this information in an area where you will be able to access them each day. Just like your vision and your mission, they will serve as a clear reminder that you have something important to look forward to.
- Guard this information and be careful with whom you share these ideas. You will find that not everyone will want to see you become successful.
- Set long-term goals and then break them down into smaller goals, so that you will be able to work step by step to make the process more manageable.
- Believe in yourself and your ability to do the work required.
- Be patient and understand that good things take time; you can't force them.
- Work hard and remain focused on the target at hand.
- Push forward with your plans, and don't get frustrated if things aren't working out as quickly as you would like.
- Think positively, even when there are obstacles in your way, and don't ever give up!

Over the years, as I've pursued my education and throughout my career, I developed a habit of setting goals, breaking them down into smaller goals, and working steadfastly towards achieving them. I've challenged myself and found ways to enjoy whatever I was doing. Most of all, I was never afraid of taking on new responsibilities or tackling what seemed like monumental tasks. Even during difficult times, I was determined to do a good job, and I held on to my belief that God was preparing me for something greater. I did not sit down and focus on what was happening at the present time; instead, I began to focus on the direction in which I wanted to go. By keeping an attitude of positivity, I was able to change my obstacles into opportunities. I encourage you to do the same, because being able to focus on where you are heading is certainly the best way to achieve your goals.

I would like to share a story about an experience on the job years ago, which took a lot of courage for me to be able to overcome my obstacles. I was working as an executive assistant for a huge organization. In the beginning, my supervisor and I had a very good working relationship. But by the end of the second year, things took a drastic turn for the worse, and she decided that I had to be terminated. I could not believe what was happening; I fought for my life because I knew that I'd not done anything wrong. After two or three weeks of harassment and intimidation, I decided that it was time to move on. She did everything to block my transfer to a different department. I had no choice but to take my complaint to the head of the organization. To my surprise, even though he was shocked to hear the details of my complaint, he was pleased that I came to meet with him. He reassured me that I would not lose my job, and he also mentioned that he was impressed with my work. For more than a year, I had worked on two huge projects which helped the organization to secure large amounts of funding, but I had not thought much of it and simply considered it part of my job. I had no idea he was paying such close attention to the work I was doing.

At the end of our discussion, he offered me a promotion to start up a new department. When he asked if I was up to the challenge, I did not hesitate and quickly said yes. I left his office feeling as if I was in the middle of a dream. I went home and began to do my research to prepare myself for this new job, which I would start the next week. Once I received the job description and settled into my new office, I immediately began to set goals for myself and the department. I later developed a plan of action because I wanted to be successful. This turned out to be one of the best experiences of my career. It was here that I decided to set new goals and a plan of action for my education; this process later resulted in me obtaining my doctoral degree.

As I write about this important lesson of setting goals and developing a plan of action, I am also reminded of the great Jamaican Olympian Usain Bolt. At just twenty-one years of age, he was responsible for shattering world records in both the 100- and 200-metre track and field events during the Summer Olympics in Beijing in 2008. He dedicated most of his time to his training because he had a lofty goal in mind. He was already well-known for his speed in the 200-metre race and had originally set out to run just that one race. However, he wanted to challenge himself. After only one year of training, he decided to run both the 200-metre and the 100-metre. This did not happen automatically simply because he wanted to. He had to plead with his coach over and over again so that the coach would buy into this idea.

On August 16, 2008, we gathered together family and friends to watch the Beijing Olympics on television. When it was time for the 100-metre finals, there were thousands of people in the stadium and millions around the world watching on television and cheering on their teams. After the sound of the gun, this athlete bolted to the finish line with lightning speed. He ran the race with such ease, even slowing down about fifteen metres from the finish line, winning in 9.69 seconds and setting a new world record. The spectators were stunned! Who would have thought that a young man from the small island of Jamaica could accomplish such a feat? One could say the odds were against him: Jamaica didn't have a state-of-the-art training centre with fancy equipment. Yet he was able to make the most out of the resources available to him. The 100-metre race was not even his area of expertise, but he trained hard and was confident that he could be successful. It was quite obvious that he had set measurable goals for himself. His daily training, passion for the sport, discipline, and dedication gave him the edge over the other competitors. Four days later at the 200-metre finals, there was excitement everywhere. Sports fans around the world and in the stadium were holding their collective breath as they waited with great anticipation for the race. The athletes positioned themselves, and as the starter's gun went off, Usain bolted from the starting line and flew down the track, leaving a measurable distance between him and the other athletes. He would set a new world record of 19.30, shattering the twelve-year-old record of 19.32 set by US track and field star Michael Johnson, who watched from the sidelines in amazement. Usain Bolt and his team later won the 4×100-metre relay in a record time of 37.10 seconds. The crowd roared as they watched Usain dance and flex his arms in his signature pose.

Everyone but Usain was astonished. Many thought it was impossible. But Usain believed in himself and was confident in his ability to win, because he knew how hard he had trained. He also knew in his heart that he had to challenge himself and was willing to attempt what others thought was impossible. This athlete had a goal in mind and a plan of action, which he had executed. He was physically and mentally prepared. Not only was this historic victory important for Usain and the people of Jamaica, but it served as a visual lesson for people all around the world. The victory showed that success is about setting realistic goals and having the strength and conviction to move forward with tenacity and great determination.

Usain Bolt has won numerous track and field events since the Beijing Olympics, and he even shattered his own record, completing the 100-metre race in 9.58 seconds in the 2009 world championships in Berlin. At the 2012 Olympics in London, thousands of people filled the stadium, and millions were glued to their television sets once more, just to watch this great Olympian sprint to the finish line in record time. These Olympic Games showcased the power of the human spirit, allowing us to witness how dedication, hard work, true grit, and perseverance can propel someone in pursuit of his dreams. Today he continues to light up the stadiums at various world championship track and field games. There is no doubt that he will go on to win many more races and set world records along the way. Some people describe him as the greatest Olympian ever, and the people in Jamaica consider him a national hero.

Human beings can accomplish anything to which they set their minds. Just like Usain Bolt, you can become passionate about your heart's desires. All you have to do is believe in yourself and make a commitment to do that which others might consider impossible. Life holds for us infinite possibilities, yet people sometimes tend to set too many limits for themselves. If you have a dream career, find someone who has already accomplished that dream and learn his story. Get as much information as you can to help you learn how he became successful. If possible, try to contact that person. If the person is a celebrity, you may feel a bit intimidated, but remember that we're all human beings. In most instances many people are flattered because others see them as role models. You would be surprised how many would honour a request for advice. While conducting your research, you may even begin to notice that some of the qualities you admire in this person are the very same qualities you possess!

We all set goals in life. Some of us talk about it while others work quietly. As you set your goals and develop your plan of action, take the time to look at the world through different lenses. Change your attitude towards life and don't be afraid to do something that is outside of your comfort zone. Jim Rohn, the famous business philosopher said, "If you don't design your own life plan, chances are you'll fall into someone else's plan and guess what they have planned for you? Not much." I believe that the more resolute you are about your goals, the more effective you'll become in achieving them. Create new habits for yourself each day, and make good choices; think outside of the box and inspire others to follow. God took just as much time to create you as he did to create a track star, so be a person of excellence and don't ever settle for mediocrity in anything you do. Working towards achieving your goals is a process. Henry David Thoreau said, "What you get by achieving your goals is not as important as what you become by achieving your goals." Work hard, work smart, and remain committed—and you will be successful. Develop your vision and your mission, and set realistic and measurable goals. Develop strategies to accomplish them and use these principles of success to validate your personal destination.

Good character is not a gift or a talent. It is something you develop step by step, and over time, based on the principles by which you choose to live. In essence, it is a firm foundation upon which your reputation lies.

Lesson 3: Develop Good Character

One of the main things evidenced by the choices you make in your daily lives is your character. Character can be defined in many ways, but it's summed up as distinctive qualities, values, and habits by which a person is known. One of the most important displays of good character is being gracious even if others do not reciprocate. Know that you are responsible for yourself and that you cannot control the actions of others. Put your heart into everything you do, and don't get discouraged if things don't always work out the way you've planned it. Develop good relationships with others, and always remember that good character leads to success. As you develop these relationships, it is important to keep your word. Your word is your bond, and so there will always be people who are counting on you. It is good to know that people have faith in you and can trust you to finish the things you set out to do. The scripture in Matthew 12:37 states, "For by thy words thou shalt be justified, and by thy words thou shalt be condemned."

As you build relationships, don't ever compromise your culture, faith, or beliefs. This principle can be a difficult, constant struggle considering the environment in which we live today. Be strong and live by the good moral and ethical principles of your cultural background—these are the things which make you who you are today, and you should be proud. Be confident in all that you do, encourage others to be their best, and model good behaviour for those around you. If you find that you start doubting yourself, lean on the word of God, knowing that with him all things are possible. Jeremiah 10:23 reminds us that we are not alone in the decisions we make.

Surround yourself with family and friends who love and care for you, and who are willing to embrace your ideas. Don't allow negative comments to throw you off track. In order to experience your true purpose in life, you have to wake up from what might seem like a bad dream, shaking off the things that are holding you down. Be courageous and understand that God did not set any limits on the things you are capable of doing, so you shouldn't set any for yourself. Have the courage to be vulnerable, because this can certainly help to transform the way you live your life. Learn to be happy with the simple things in life, and don't ever allow the things you have accumulated to define your success. That's not what success is all about. Until you are able to get to that place where you truly feel happy with yourself and the life you are living, you will not be able to realize your true potential or to see how successful you really are.

In this world today, with so many temptations around you, being able to develop a good character is paramount. What you do today will not only affect you now but will have an impact on your life in the future, and so when things do not work out the way you expect them to, don't rush to change things. Be honest with those around you and don't ever give up. I remember reading a quote by Thomas Macaulay which states, "The measure of a man's real character is what he would do if he knew he would never be found out." I consider this to be a very profound statement, because I believe that honesty is certainly the best policy. As you make plans to move forward with your ideas, take a little time to sit back and think before you act. Remain calm and positive. Take responsibility for your actions and then plan new strategies to move forward. This might be a time when you need your family and friends, so always be loving and kind to them, treating them with respect. Good character is not a gift or a talent; it is something you develop step by step and over time, based on the principles by which you choose to live. In essence, it is a firm foundation upon which your reputation lies. As you work on building your character, remember that good habits help to build good character. Here are a few character traits that will not only help you to build a good character but will also help you to be confident and live your best life.

Honesty

I'm sure you've heard that being honest is the best way to live your life. Even though sometimes you may find it difficult, it's best to stand your ground and be truthful. I believe that honesty is an admirable characteristic because it's genuine and garners trust. Nothing is greater than being able to trust someone. Whether you are in school, on the job, or in a relationship, you will be faced with situations where you might be tempted to tell a lie or alter the truth to avoid being caught, and you may think that no one is going to find out. But it doesn't always happen the way you planned it. The act of lying and cheating can become addictive. Sometimes you may find that you'll have to create a lie to cover the first lie you told, and then another. In the end, that lie grows exponentially, and you'll be caught up into a web of lies. Before you know it, you've developed a habit of being dishonest, and people will no longer trust you or believe anything you say.

I remember that when I taught a high school reading class, it was challenging to work with some of the students. But at the same time I was determined to see this particular group of students succeed. They had failed the class before and were such a rowdy bunch that no one wanted to teach them. When I was approached to do the job, I hesitated for a moment but felt that I owed it to myself to take on this challenge. Of course I was ready to quit after the first period, but after I called my daughter, she reminded me that they were teenagers and encouraged me to hang in there, and I did. We worked hard on various projects throughout the school year, and I began to see some improvement.

For the end-of-year project, they were given an assignment which would account for a large portion of their grade. The assignment consisted of reading a novel of their choice, writing chapter summaries, conducting interviews, and making presentations to the class. They were given opportunities to utilize the media room and library in order to do research and type their papers. They were constantly reminded of the deadlines for each section of the project and how important it was to do their own work. I also made myself available for one-on-one instruction and assistance.

At the end of the project, when it was time to turn in the written summaries, I was surprised to see one particular student turning in her work on time. She had never done this before, and I'd always suspected that she had someone else doing her assignments. However, I was not able to prove it. This time, the way the assignment was written, it raised a red flag for me. It was neatly put together, and I was impressed. After grading a few papers, I decided to read it carefully. After reading the first two paragraphs, I stopped. Somehow this did not sound like the person I knew, and so I decided to check the Internet. I was surprised to see that she had just copied all of her summaries directly from the Internet. The next day I called the student to my desk and told her that what she did was wrong and that it was not worth it to jeopardize a whole year's work by cheating. At first she denied it, but then she became agitated and said to me, "Miss, how did you find out?" This was an admission of guilt right there. I took the time to remind her that it is best to be honest at all times, because one's destiny is determined by one's character.

Cheating in class may not seem like a big deal, but you'll be surprised at how quickly and easily a little transgression can turn into a big deal. Even more disconcerting is the feeling you get when you happen to get away with something. It makes you want to do it again, thereby developing a habit of being dishonest. We all know that a credit got by a lie will only last for a short time because someone will certainly find out. Therefore, it is important to develop good habits and be honest at all times, understanding that though others may not be watching, being deceitful is essentially doing yourself a disservice. Being honourable is tantamount. Be sincere, tell the truth, and don't mislead others. When you develop good habits, you are preparing yourself for excellence. The decisions you make day by day will reflect your true character. In the end success depends on who you are and not necessarily what you do.

Integrity

Honesty and integrity go hand in hand, and so it's important to live according to good moral and ethical principles—and honesty of purpose. Don't be afraid to set high standards for yourself and to strive to always do what is right. Live a life that is better than what others expect of you. When you set out to do something, don't do it because you want to please your friends or the people on the job. Instead, be true to yourself, and they will respect you. This may be your only opportunity to make a difference. In the end, your actions will not only make you feel good about what you've done, but they will help others to see you for who you are. This will eventually become an expression of what you believe in. As Shakespeare said in *Hamlet*, "This above all: to thine own self be true, and it must follow as the night the day, thou canst not then be false to any man."

Integrity counts in all aspects of life, and so it is important to have passion for what you believe in and to encourage others to do the same. Sometimes you'll find that you are presented with a difficult task. Whenever this happens, don't try to take the easy route just because you cannot be bothered to do the work required. Successful people don't achieve their goals by taking shortcuts; instead, they get to work early, and occasionally they stay late to get the job done. The principle applies to school or any other applicable situation. Do not submit yourself to cutting corners just to get it over with. In everything you do, you should aim to set a good example for others to follow and to be sincere with others and yourself. Give 100 per cent effort to every assignment because a mediocre job is a sign of laziness. Let's face it: you can't always dodge the bullet; one day it will ricochet and hit you where it hurts.

Some of the most powerful lessons I've learned over the years were instilled in me by Mr. C. L. Stuart, the headmaster of my high school in Jamaica. He was admired by many as a man of principle, and he was very keen on making students' educational experience an enriching preparation for life. He would not and could not stand for mediocrity. He counselled us daily and encouraged us to strive for excellence, using the resources we had to make the most of life's opportunities. Our high school motto was and still is "Perstare et Praestare", which means "Persevere and Excel". We understood the importance of working hard to produce quality work, as well as the need to do it on our own. The rules were quite clear: dishonesty was unacceptable and could result in expulsion. As children these words of wisdom and encouragement inspired us to do our best at all times. We understood that in order to achieve our educational goals, we had to work hard and do what was necessary to prepare for our examinations. Over the years these life lessons have been the cornerstone of my educational, professional, and personal life experiences, and I will never forget them.

I believe that everyone can learn something from other people's experiences. I encourage you to be honest in all that you do, keep your word, honour your commitments, and aim to be a person of excellence and integrity. This approach will allow you to gain trust and commitment from others. Always treat people with respect and kindness; find ways to be a blessing to them. I implore you to hold on to something that will inspire you to do well. Set high moral principles in your life, personally and professionally, and stick by them. Listen to your conscience, your inner voice, and do the right thing at all times. Develop a sense of curiosity, both in school and on the job, because it's great to find out what's going on around you. This curiosity will allow you to determine whether or not you are happy with what you are doing. I've said this before, but I will repeat it because it is that important: be true to yourself and know who you are.

You should see yourself as someone special, and know that you are destined to do great things. Think positive and don't allow negative thoughts to prevent you from living up to your true potential. When things get rough, don't try to change yourself to fit the situation. Instead, change your view of the experience, keeping in mind that from every experience there is a lesson to be learned. Be your best by living your life and doing things with honesty, integrity, and compassion. In doing so, you'll teach people how to treat you.

Compassion

Being compassionate is a strong and admirable character trait. It may be also one of the hardest, because humans tend to be innately selfish. We naturally do things and seek things that benefit ourselves. Being compassionate requires you to put others first. As you journey through life, you will come across people who need a helping hand. It is times like these when you will need to show compassion by listening to them, trying to understand their needs, helping if you can, and encouraging them to be brave and strong. When you go out of your way to be kind to others, not only will you be blessed, but this kindness might even become contagious with others around you. Try it out for yourself and see what happens. It can even be as simple as sharing a smile with someone to help brighten their day; you will find that somehow others can't help but smile back at you, or someone else. You will also notice that the feeling you get from smiling and seeing others smile back is priceless! When speaking with other people, learn to listen actively and look them in the eye; this shows that you believe what they are saying is important. If you are able to take the time to perform one small deed each day for someone in need, then this may lead to the gradual engenderment of great happiness, and you will certainly live a fulfilled life. In the words of Mark Twain, "Kindness is a language which the deaf can hear and the blind can read."

You can also show compassion by being thoughtful, generous, and kind. But more important, you can show compassion by simply being there, by taking the time to lend an ear or a shoulder to someone who is going through a difficult time. Even if you don't know what to say or how to console someone, just being able to listen and showing that you care can make a difference. Sometimes your mere presence is what's important. Don't just tell people that you care—*show* them that you care. Your deeds and actions will be a testament of your character, and you never know when you may need someone to do the same for you.

Becoming a volunteer at some point in your life is a good way to show compassion. Get involved in your community and give back to those in need. These personal habits will help to strengthen your character and also make you a better person. You can consider it to be an opportunity to show love to others by being of service to them. Being kind is like an emotional bandage in times of sorrow: it helps to heal hearts and soothe pain. When a child is hurt, he feels good knowing that his mother will be there to kiss away the pain, but the best feeling of all is when she covers that cut with a bandage. Then the pain suddenly disappears, and the child is able to move on and play once more. Show some kindness without expecting something in return. If you are able to give freely and unselfishly, not only will you be a blessing to someone, but blessings will be bestowed upon you.

Being compassionate also requires you to manage your emotions differently. Be courteous, polite, and respectful to others; treat others fairly and try not to be judgmental. Throughout your life you will meet many different types of people. You will meet some whom you admire and some whom you despise. You will not get along with everyone, and you will have disagreements. Don't allow the negative comments to become so ingrained in your thinking that they prevent you from achieving your goals. Better yet, don't hold on to the painful experiences from the past, because that will cause much stress in your life. Instead, learn to forgive and move on. Forgiveness is a very powerful act in that it conveys a message of compassion, and God will bless you as you forgive others. If you find yourself getting angry at people because they did something wrong or maybe even insulted you, take the high road and walk away. It may be tempting to berate, belittle, and give them a good chastising, but words spoken in anger can be hurtful; once you say them, you will never be able to take them back. Harmful words can continue to pierce through the soul for a very long time. They can ruin friendships and relationships, and it can take the person who is hurt a very long time to recover. But words spoken with love and compassion can persuade others to see things from a different perspective, or help to be a source of healing and encouragement. Proverbs 15:1 states, "A soft answer turneth away wrath, but grievous words stir up anger."

Courage

Throughout our lives, we will all be faced with challenges, some big and some small. No one is exempt from this. You will have challenges in school, in your career, and in your personal lives. It's easy to become fearful and doubtful, thinking you will not succeed. But what matters most is your attitude and how you handle these situations. Being courageous is an art. When the chips are down, stand firm and have the confidence to be completely yourself. You should see yourself as strong, valuable, and talented. If you have enough courage to look past what's wrong and to focus on what's right, then success is well within your reach. Whatever you do, don't allow that element of fear to become the barrier to your success. Say, "I've got this!" Then step out in faith and allow God to lead. God challenges us to make us stronger, and he prepares us to overcome our doubts and fears of the future. Sometimes we simply have to wait a bit longer. Practice praying and being patient, knowing that when you ask for something in prayer, you should believe that God will answer.

We start out as children, with our parents taking care of us and making decisions for us. When we get older, we must learn how to make decisions for ourselves. As you continue on your journey through life, you will learn how to be courageous and make choices that will affect you as well as others around you. Get involved in doing something that will help to change someone's life. When you sit back and don't get involved, you show no courage. But when you stand up, or step out of your comfort zone, and do something which you or others thought you would not be able to do, this is a good sign of courage; it shows that you are taking a step forward towards making a difference. In order to be successful, it is important for you to know who you are and know your purpose in life. You will have to be confident, believe in yourself, and stand firm for that which you actually believe. With this confidence you will find that everything you think, feel, and do is in divine order and is part of the universal flow that helps you discover who you really are. God knows the desires of our hearts, and he wants the best for each and every one of us. He has a plan for our lives, and he has a way of using us to do extraordinary things even when we think that we are not capable of doing so.

I would like to tell you a story about a young man I know quite well. With almost one year to go before graduating from high school, he was faced with eviction by his family. It was not because he was a bad son or a bad student, but simply because his parents had left him as a child, and he was now becoming a burden to his grandparents; they were now much older and could no longer afford to take care of him. They, along with their family and friends, thought he was old enough to quit school and find a job. One can imagine how devastating this was for him. At age seventeen he had nowhere to go and did not wish to become a burden to anyone else. For him, his education was his only path to success, and he could not see himself dropping out of school. He had a few months left before graduation and simply needed a place to stay. He went to classes for the next two weeks, doing all that was required of him, but deep down he was wondering how he was going to make it for the rest of the school year.

Time went by, and after sneaking in and out of the house to go to school and pretending that he was looking for a job, he could no longer do this. He made the conscious decision to leave home because he was not able to live there in peace anymore.

It so happened that I was scheduled to visit his school, and I requested to have a meeting with him. I was his mentor, but I had no idea this was happening. As we sat there talking, I could tell by the look on his face that something was bothering him, and so I decided to ask. He told me his story and then mentioned that he was staying in an abandoned house. I was so shocked that I became speechless. I was more scared for him than he was for himself. He began to console *me* and told me not to worry, because even though he was taking a risk by being there, no one would ever find out. He mentioned that each day he mustered the courage to go to school and was able to blend in with everyone as though everything was okay. He found ways to get food to eat and a place to sleep, and he was able to take care of his laundry. After taking some time to absorb what he was saying to me, I began to admire his courage and knew that something had to be done.

With the help of a friend, he was able to move into a nice home with people who truly cared for him. They were generous and kind, and they also understood the importance of a good education. He later graduated from high school and went on to college where he earned a bachelor's degree. Today he is doing well, has a very good job and his own apartment, and is currently pursuing a master's degree. But most of all he has not forgotten where he came from or the people who were there to help him, including his grandparents. We continue to have a very special relationship. I admire his courage. I strongly believe that when you see someone in trouble who needs a helping hand, you cannot sit back and not get involved. You have to show some courage by standing up and doing something to help make a difference.

When we think about courage, it is necessary to point out that courage is the most important virtue of all. It is an essential ingredient for one's success and personal development. This young man is an example of someone who displayed great courage when almost everything was taken away from him. He was able to face the difficulties and dangers that lie ahead without fear; even though he knew deep down that one day he could be caught, he did it anyway. He showed courage by separating from his family at a young age. Even without the comfort of home or the resources he needed, he was determined to follow his dream of obtaining a good education. He showed courage through this experience by looking fear in the face and dealing with it, knowing that if he was able to make it through these difficult times, he would be able to handle whatever came after. He had the strength and the resolve to face those difficult and painful situations head-on, because he believed in himself and his dream.

There will come a time when you will get to a place where your life feels empty or unfulfilled, and you'll feel like giving up or walking away. We have all been there at some point or another. It is at this moment that you will need to find the courage to stay the course, follow your heart's deepest desires, and have the courage to do what you truly love. If you are not doing something you feel passionate about, you will ultimately become unhappy and feel as though a little part of you is slipping away every day. In order to be courageous, you have to be vulnerable. Learn to let go of the fear and emotional hang-ups in your life, and allow yourself that time and space to be creative. It is in this moment that you will build up the courage to do what really needs to be done in order to get over the fear. Once again, don't allow the negative opinions of others to block your thoughts and ideas. Instead, be vigilant about your beliefs and push ahead, and in the end you might just leave a lasting impression on others.

Great leaders have a clear vision and lead with a sense of purpose. They lead by example and are able to inspire and influence others to be their best.

Lesson 4: Develop Good Leadership Skills

Leadership is truly a labour of love. In order to be considered a good leader, you have to be willing to take on the many responsibilities leadership entails, and you must develop good leadership skills. You have to be confident, knowing that there are people who count on you and that you cannot disappoint them. You'll need to have that personal conviction and believe strongly in whatever you set out to do. As a leader you'll have to understand that you are there to give of yourself, to serve, because service is a fundamental part of your role as a leader. It is important to understand that as you lead, you are not just serving the company, a group, or an organization—essentially, you are serving the people. They could be your staff, the stakeholders, or the community. These are people who will look to you for guidance and leadership. As a leader you will find that sometimes things can become difficult and very challenging; you might even begin to feel emotionally or spiritually drained. It is then that you will need to turn to the scriptures for strength and guidance, because they never fail. Isaiah 42:16 states, "And I will bring the blind by a way that they knew not; I will lead them in paths that they have not known: I will make darkness light before them, and crooked things straight. These things I will do unto them, and not forsake them."

It is possible that many of you are in leadership positions at this moment. You should be congratulated because this is an awesome responsibility, and you should be proud of the accomplishment. Whenever you make the choice to lead—whether it's on the job, in the classroom, on the sports field, or in your community—you are choosing to make a commitment to getting something done. One of the ways in which a leader can be successful is by setting goals, having the discipline to prioritize them, and having the ability to work towards achieving them. Sometimes in life when you want something badly, you have to learn to stay focused and tackle things one task at a time. We can accomplish anything we set out to do as long as we believe in ourselves and have that burning desire to see our dreams become a reality.

I remember growing up in a community in Jamaica where we did not have a playing field. The children played soccer and cricket and ran track on a grassy field that was owned by one of the neighbours. When it was time for a local election, one of the leaders in my community promised that he would ensure that the kids in the community had a safe place to play. He said that was at the top of his list of priorities for the people if they would vote for him on the day of elections. Members of the community were excited, and so they were very happy to elect him as their leader. After the elections were over, he won, and it did not take him very long before he kept his promise. He built a community centre equipped with all the necessary resources, and he purchased the extra land so that children would have ample space to play.

The people in the community and surrounding areas were very happy. They saw him as the best leader they'd ever had because he stuck to his word and honoured his commitment. Even though it was not a fancy stadium because funds were not available for that, he made a promise and knew that the people were counting on him to deliver. It was important not to let them down. All eyes were on him, and this was the time to show the people that they could take him at his word. Because of his commitment to serving the people in his community, he was elected over and over again. People grew to trust him and believed in his vision for the community.

As you lead, set the standards by which you wish to lead and stick to them, and others will respect you, have confidence in you, and follow you. You never know how much influence you have in someone else's life. It is also good to remember that if no one is willing to follow you, then you are not a good leader. A good leader is one who leads by setting the example instead of following others, and who displays a positive attitude. A good leader knows when to take authority, is honest with his people, and is committed to the cause. As a leader, you have to show courage in the face of adversity and make a bold statement. You will never be able to have a big impact on the people around you if you are not willing to say what's on your mind, even if it's not what others want to hear. Let's face it—it's your life and your vision, and you can't please everyone.

Have the courage to do something different by taking things one step at a time. Whatever you set out to do, it must be done with intention and clarity. When you have that depth of clarity to listen to your own instinct (that inner voice) and to do what is necessary, then you will become the person you ought to be. Be true to yourself and move forward in faith, knowing that God has cleared a path for you not only to achieve your goal but to be the best in whatever you do. As you move ahead, dig deep, dare to be courageous, and have big bold dreams for the future. Never stop daring to be great! God will connect you with all of the resources you will need in order to be successful.

As a leader it is important to remember that you are influencing others. The people around you are looking for someone who has the heart and mind to commit so that they will eventually be influenced by you. People aren't looking for someone to dictate their every move; instead, they will be looking to you for guidance, clarification, and inspiration. Learn to respect the people around you, accept them for who they are, and meet them where they are in life. You might just be the one to encourage them and inspire them to move forward and make changes in their lives. Great leaders have a clear vision and lead with a sense of purpose; they lead by setting the pace and are able to inspire and influence others to be their best. As you go about your daily life, display a positive attitude, be personable, connect with the people around you, and relate to them as individuals. They would like to know that you are someone with whom they can have a conversation, that you are someone whom they can trust. When you are able to show that you care about the people on your team, they in turn will feel good about themselves while they are in your presence. Therefore, don't go around being too serious all the time. Lighten up a bit and display the type of attitude which will make them feel comfortable talking with you.

Invite the members of your team to meet with you to discuss their ideas or concerns, and show interest in the conversations. When they leave the room, they want to feel as though they were heard. They would also like to leave the meeting believing that what they had to contribute to the conversation was important. Being able to influence others and connect with them is a good sign of leadership; this is done through good communication, transparency, and treating others with respect. Learning to communicate effectively with people at all levels is also a sign of good leadership. By creating a safe place for people to be able to communicate with you and others, you're creating a sense of direction for the future. It was Lou Gerstner, former CEO of IBM, who once said, "Leaders get people to do things they otherwise wouldn't do. Leaders create a sense of urgency for the future. It's about communication, transparency, and treating others as equals."

There are many misconceptions about leadership, and it's important to understand that when you lead, things can become complicated. However, in order to achieve success as a leader, here are a few important tips for you to consider.

- Believe in yourself and be confident in your ability to lead. These are two of the qualities that might help you get tapped for leadership positions.
- Learn how to be flexible and amenable to change. A willingness to accept change is a sign of growth.

- Participate in leadership-training seminars and read good books on leadership, because everything you need to know as a leader cannot be learned overnight.
- Learn how to be an effective change agent; this will help you to get things done.
- Show respect to others around you, especially those on your team.
- Show emotional strength and lead from the heart.
- Build strong relationships with individuals who look to you for leadership, and inspire them to be the best they can be.
- Get to know the people on your team, respect their ideas, and take good care of them. Every good leader needs to know that there is a team of people he or she can count on, and in order to build this team, it has to be done one by one.
- Develop a good attitude and be supportive of your peers and of the members of your team.
- Maintain that connection with your inner self, and don't allow others to sway you or distract you from what your heart or your instinct is telling you to do.
- Be confident in the decisions you make; as you lead, understand that strength and conviction are important.
- Put your heart and soul into whatever you do, and take responsibility for your actions. The people around you will respect you because you stepped up to the plate when it was necessary.

These are some of the qualities of a good leader which will help to inspire others around you. If you display any form of self-doubt, it will eventually destroy your confidence. John Maxwell, one of America's experts on leadership, said, "A leader is one who knows the way, goes the way, and shows the way."

With the changing demographics, and our society's growing diversity, it is necessary for leaders to learn how to work with people from all walks of life. You have to learn about the histories, cultures, languages, needs, and challenges of the people who live and work around you. You have to learn to be culturally sensitive and how to be tolerant and respectful of other people's diversity. A good leader should realize that people are different and that we all come from various cultural backgrounds. We carry with us unique strengths and abilities that, when put together, can form a mighty force. In order to accomplish your goals, you will be required to use your skills to mobilize the talents and energies of the people around you. Therefore, if you are in a position where you will need to form a team, be careful how you choose the members of this team. The person you leave behind might just be the one that has the ability to take your team to the next level.

As you get to know the people around you, it will become easier for you to identify who you can trust. Empower the good people on your team and place them in good positions. You will certainly find this to be very rewarding. No matter what type of leadership position in which you find yourself, take time to serve as a mentor to a fellow co-worker, or even to a student. Because you are in this position, people look up to you and respect you. Be humble and show compassion when necessary. Teach by example and allow others to see how passionate you are about what you believe. You never know how much impact you can have on another person's life until you spend some time with them. Who knows—you might find this to be a very rewarding experience.

Leadership should not be considered a title or even a privilege. Instead, it should be seen as one of the greatest responsibilities of your life. As you carry out these responsibilities, you should understand that your personal character is very important. Therefore, surround yourself with people of good character because your reputation will always be on the line. It is a well-known fact that an effective leader is not someone who is always loved or admired, so be prepared for that. You will be highly visible, and so you should be of good moral character, lead from your heart, and lead by setting a good example. As a leader, it is important to be vulnerable at the right time. This allows the people around you to see your true and authentic self. You will need to stick to your core values and instill in others a sense of respect, dignity, compassion, and a sense of community. As long as you are honest, people will believe in you and follow you. Whatever the situation might be, you should be confident about the decisions you've made, because in the end you have to be able to look yourself in the mirror and know that your integrity is intact.

It is clear that being a leader is not easy. But whatever you do, don't allow work, computers, cell phones, and other electronic gadgets to hijack your life. Remember that nothing in life is permanent—not even life itself. We are all here temporarily, and as a result we need to make the best use of each day that is loaned to us. Create a balance between your work and your personal life, and spend time with your family. When faced with difficult situations, remember to pray, study, and obey the word of God, because it will give you strength to face the difficulties and challenges in life. Whenever you need to find the answer to questions or figure things out for yourself, read books written by (as well as books about) great leaders like Martin Luther King Jr. and Mohandas "Mahatma" Gandhi, two great civil rights leaders. Also, don't forget other great leaders such as Eleanor Roosevelt, who fought for the rights of women and African Americans, as well as many other important issues. Most of all, don't forget the Holy Bible, the greatest book of all that will teach you all you need to know about leadership, because of Jesus being the greatest leader of all times. In teaching people how to model a kind and loving leadership style, Laurie Beth Jones once said, "Jesus did not follow the crowd. He led it. He did not report the news. He made it happen." It is up to you to look at the list of great leaders and find out what made them successful. Learning more about them will help you to grow and develop your leadership skills. As you study these people, you will eventually develop your own unique leadership style, which will allow you to lead with a sense of purpose.

Be grateful for the things you have in your life. Appreciate your family and friends, knowing that if you appreciate and care for them, they will add value to your life.

Lesson 5: Be Grateful

There are so many things in life that we take for granted each day, when we should really be grateful. When you awake each morning, give thanks to God for his many blessings and for allowing you to live to see another sunrise. Think of the fullness of your life and be grateful to him for granting you all that you have. Whenever you feel down and out, try to find something to be grateful for. Be grateful that you are surrounded by people who love you and care for you. Each day learn to be grateful for the fact that you are alive and walking. Develop an attitude of faith, knowing that the God who brought you to this point will take you through any difficulties you may encounter. If you have faith in God, it will allow you to experience infinite possibilities and grant your soul the freedom to soar. The scripture is replete with references to underscore the simple fact that God will show us his favour if we remain faithful and are grateful for the things we have, big and small. Hebrews 11:1 tells us clearly, "Faith is the substance of things hoped for, the evidence of things not seen."

Gratitude is a key component of leadership, and being faithful and thankful for all that we have is a good way to start the day. You will face challenges in life, and sometimes you will feel like giving up. But if you take the time to look around you, you will find that despite these challenges, there are many things for which you should be grateful. Many of you have food, shelter, family, and friends who care for you—and the list goes on.

Instead of complaining about the fact that things are not working out the way you would like, why not pause for a moment and count your blessings? Think about those people who are suffering in other countries. There is violence everywhere around them, and sometimes they witness family members being killed right in front of their eyes. While this is happening, you are safe where you live. These people have no electricity, no medical facilities, no access to simple first aid, and not even access to clean water. Stop and think of the thousands whose countries have been devastated by natural disasters. Many people have lost limbs and even their families. They have no roof over their heads, no food to eat, no clothes to wear, and no schools for the children to attend. And yet despite all of this tragedy, they are grateful because they are alive. Instead of walking with your head in the clouds, take a good look around you. There are many people right there in your own community who have lost their jobs and their homes, yet they are grateful for life and have hope for the future. As you think on these things, count your blessings and be thankful for all that you have, knowing that you can always rewrite new chapters to your life's story. If you think on these things and have a grateful heart, then you will realize how blessed you are.

As you journey through life, learn to appreciate your family and friends, knowing that if you appreciate and care for them, then in turn they will add value to your life. Respect them and be grateful for the relationships you have with them. If those relationships are not as you would like them to be, then do something about it. Take time out to spend with family and friends who mean a lot to you, and learn to be thankful for the small things in life as well as the big things. Some of you have spent years in school studying, and you've worked hard at your job in order to be successful. Therefore, you should be grateful that you had the opportunity to attend school, get an education, and now have a good job. Be grateful for the things you have been able to accomplish in life and learn how to celebrate your achievements, because you've earned it. As you celebrate, don't forget to thank the people who've helped you along the way. But most of all, you should be thankful to God for his mercies, which endure forever. It is always important to remember where you are coming from, because this will help to pave the way for where you are going. Once you have a sense of gratitude, you'll be able to see things through different lenses and appreciate the life you're living. The great author and poet Maya Angelou would say, "Maintain an attitude of gratitude."

In times of difficulties when you're feeling stressed or depressed, don't be afraid. You have to learn to be vulnerable and ask for help. Allow others into your life so that they will be able to experience the joy of giving and sharing. The fact that you were able to ask for help could become a profound and life-changing experience for you. Every now and then we all need what I call a mental health break. Take the time to meditate and listen to some inspirational music that will soothe your soul and calm your mind. Escape from all the noise and distractions; be present in the moment. Wait in the stillness so you can relax, connect with the spirit, and be at peace with yourself. Meditation is so powerful that many spiritual leaders such as Dr. Deepak Chopra and Dr. Wayne Dyer use it as the cornerstone of their teachings. Meditation not only helps to relieve stress, which is one of the main problems facing so many people in our society, but it also helps to open up the door to your soul and your spirituality. When you meditate in the silence, that is when you'll find that you have the time to think and also become very creative. Meditation may not be for everyone, but it is considered to be a means by which one can regain one's strength.

Because of all the stress in the world, it is important to take a few moments to breathe and allow peaceful thoughts into your mind. Take a moment to close your eyes and imagine that you are alone in a room and that there is no noise or anyone around you. Take the time to breathe slowly, relax, and feel the difference. As you meditate, you will be able to listen to that inner voice and realize the many blessings God has in store for you. In this quietness you will feel free, and you will be able to find strength to overcome your fears and handle whatever is causing the stress. Psalm 46:10 encourages us to take some time to be quiet and be alone with the spirit: "Be still and know that I am God." Open up your mind and your heart to experience new and exciting things. Live a life that is pleasing to God, and you will be surprised at the changes he will make in your life. Each day, focus on the word of God for renewed strength. Be grateful for his blessings and adopt a more positive approach to life. As you go about your daily business, be grateful for what you have and do not complain or sweat the small stuff. Instead of going around complaining, stay focused, change your attitude to one of gratitude, and express that gratitude by being kind to others. Take the time to perform an act of kindness to someone less fortunate than you are. You will find that the more you take time to be of service to others, the more you will see how happy you've become. You'll even realize that you are fulfilling your purpose in life. Even though there are a lot of misconceptions about passion, you can find passion in the things you really care about; all you need to do is stay focused, create positive energy around you by being with people who are like-minded, and find joy in whatever you're doing. Choose to be happy. Live in the moment and make each day the most beautiful day of your life. At the end of the day, don't forget to give thanks to God, the creator of the universe, for granting you life and allowing you to have so many wonderful experiences, living the life of your dreams.

Relationships are the most precious commodities anyone can have, but good relationships don't happen overnight. It takes time to get to know yourself, and to experience that joy and love within, before you'll be able to share that love with others.

Lesson 6: Build Lasting and Meaningful Relationships

Friendships

It doesn't matter how much you have in life—the fancy cars, the big homes, the great education. You cannot truly say that you are happy without good relationships. As you create relationships, it is important to value who you are, know what you want, and set the standards for how you would like to be treated. If you don't, you will be bombarded with the demands and unrealistic expectations of others. Take the time to get to know the people around you and build a real bond of friendship. Be careful how you choose your friends, because the company you keep can be seen as a reflection of who you are. Find friends who are like-minded, with whom you can associate; seek out people who are dreamers and who have a vision.

Creating meaningful friendships is a wonderful thing, but don't expect your friends to be who you want them to be. Remember that even though we are all created equal, we are all different. We have within us our own unique values, norms, and ideas of the world around us. Therefore, it is important to learn to value and appreciate your friends, and to learn from each other. In order to have a peaceful and lasting friendship, it is also important to respect each other and to treat others the way you would like to be treated. Most important, be kind and nonjudgmental. Keep a positive attitude at all times because it will allow you to gain positive results from those around you. Your attitude is expressed in everything you say or do, no matter where you are. Show genuine love and respect for your friends. Acknowledge them and make them realize that they are important in your lives. Call them out when they are wrong, but don't be afraid to compliment them for something good they have done; this will not only make them feel good about themselves, but it will show that you truly care.

Surround yourself with people who inspire you, believe in you, encourage you, lift you up, and challenge you to be the best you can be. Don't waste your time with people who are not able to add value to your life, and get rid of those who tend to drag you down. These negative people will keep you from becoming who God wants you to be and from fulfilling your purpose in life. A good friend is one who will always be there in good times and bad. It is important to cherish the friendships you've developed over the years—don't ever take your friends for granted. Always remember that friendship is a two-way street. True friendships can help to make you feel fulfilled and can bring out the joy in you. Therefore, the onus is on you to be faithful to the people you consider to be your friends. Proverbs 18:24 says, "A man that hath friends must shew himself friendly: and there is a friend that sticketh closer than a brother."

As you evolve, you will find that not all of your friends are ready to move on in a positive direction. Evaluate those who have negative intentions and don't allow their negative energy to keep you down. Remember that people don't determine your destiny— God does. Many people look to others for happiness, and that's a big mistake because later on they'll realize that the people they consider to be friends are the same ones who will end up like Brutus and betray them. Therefore, be happy with yourself and don't rely on your friends to make you happy. If they offend you, don't pretend that you are not hurting. Speak the truth at all times and understand that good relationships come with both joy and pain. Yes, the truth hurts, but it hurts you more if you keep your feelings inside. Steven Covey put it clearly when he wrote, "Our greatest joy and our greatest pain come in our relationships with others."

Good friends are there for you in good times and bad, and they do not air your dirty laundry in public; instead, they have your back. A true friend tells the truth and does it with love. Be loyal to your friends, but don't allow them to control your life. When you find that you are not satisfied with the way things are going, speak up and let them know how you're feeling. If, after telling the truth, you lose that friendship, then you'll realize that it wasn't real in the first place. In the end you'll find that you've just rid yourself of one more obstacle in your life. Now, instead of wasting time with someone who is not loving, caring, or kind, you can have more time to care for yourself, to meditate, and to pray to God for guidance. As stated in the writings of Ben Sirach (Ecclesiastes 6:5–16), a Jewish scribe from the second century BC, "A kindly turn of speech attracts new friends, a courteous tongue invites many a friendly response. Let your acquaintances be many, but for advisors choose one out of a thousand." All of this is important in order to build good, lasting, and meaningful friendships.

Intimate Relationships

As you begin to develop intimate relationships, it is important to choose wisely. Get to know the person you are interested in as much as possible, making that person feel important. Find out about family background. Learn about the person's culture, religious beliefs or spirituality, hobbies, and the things that are of interest to him or her. Understand clearly his or her likes and dislikes. If you don't take the time to do this, you might end up being sorry. Be careful not to rush into something serious until you are sure that you've done your homework and that you are truly satisfied with what you've found. Being in a relationship is a very important decision and is not one you should rush into or take lightly.

This is your life and your future, and it behoves you to be on guard and do what's necessary to ensure that you do not get your heart broken. Understand clearly that it's best to think with your head and not just your heart. Share your love with people who've earned the right to have your love—people who respect you, value your friendship, and will love you in return without conditions. Consider all that you've learned about each other. Look at the big picture, and once a decision is made to move forward with the relationship, be prepared to work hard to keep it in a positive light.

As you work on building this relationship you'll want to make sure it's a good and healthy one. First of all, it is so important for you to be good friends and show that you trust and respect each other. Commit to the relationship with love and loyalty for one another. It is always good to hear someone say that he or she loves you, but being loyal to that person you love so dearly is a crucial component in any good relationship. It means that you are committed to being with this one person and will work together to build a future filled with love, peace, and harmony. As you commit to this relationship, share your joys and your sorrows, learn from each other, honour the differences that you have, and allow it to bring out the excitement in both of you. Be affectionate yet sensitive about each other's feelings, and spend quality time together. Take the time to talk about your hopes and your dreams for the future, or whatever might be necessary to keep the relationship growing stronger. These heart-to-heart talks can help to make your partner feel important, giving him or her a sense of well-being and value, but most of all it will certainly help to put things into perspective.

As your relationship evolves, take long walks together and hold hands as you go along, because this helps you to stay connected; it is also a sign that the love is still strong. Try new things every now and then to bring some freshness into the relationship. Write letters to each other, or even a note to say how you are feeling about your partner, and post it on the mirror in the bathroom; this will certainly help to brighten your partner's day. Share special moments with each other doing simple things that you both enjoy.

I have a friend who enjoys playing soccer, and he watches the games all the time. For him, it doesn't matter where the game is being played or even if the commentators are speaking in another language. He played soccer as a young man, and therefore he understands the game very well. Over time his wife became tired of being by herself, and so she started watching the game with him. In no time at all she became interested. Now they value this time together more than ever. For them, watching the soccer game together is like watching the Super Bowl. They watch the qualifying games between the various countries and make big plans for the World Cup games. They are very passionate about their teams, and they work together around the home to get things done so that they'll never miss a game. They are participating in something they both enjoy, they spend more quality time together, and as a result they have a lot more to talk about.

Be vulnerable and let go of the fear of the unknown. A healthy relationship will prosper and develop into a strong bond if you love and respect each other as individuals, and if you are accepting of each other. In your relationship with your partner, know that you matter and find some synergy between who you are and who your friends or others would like you to be. In order for this relationship to grow and for you to feel fulfilled, there has to be a deep connection, some compatibility in the things you like to do. You will both need to develop that deep bond that is satisfying, but most of all, you need to have a true spiritual partnership—one that is equal. This is something important for you to think about.

We hear every day that good communication is a very essential ingredient for a loving and lasting relationship. Therefore, find ways to stay connected and work together through positive communication, to work things out and solve problems. Don't be afraid to take the time to ask questions when you are not sure; be careful not to criticize or argue if you do not agree with what is being said. Allow your partner to express his or her feelings, and be courteous and considerate. Whenever you are having a conversation, be careful what you say and how it is said. Words that are hurtful will only cause conflict in the relationship, and even though your partner might forgive you, he or she might never forget. Remember that good, lasting relationships do not happen overnight; it takes hard work, good communication, dedication, and compromise.

In every relationship it is very important for both parties to feel safe and able to express their feelings without being afraid of a conflict. Engaging in conversations is the most effective way to get to know your partner. In a conversation you will both have your own ideas and opinions, and you will not always agree with each other, but that's okay. Effective communication also requires good listening habits. Be authentic and learn to be a good listener. If you take the time to listen and show interest in what your partner has to say without being defensive or getting upset, it's always possible for you to learn something different. In the end not only will your partner feel respected, but you might even find out that you were right after all. Being in a relationship is not always easy, and sometimes people don't get along because they are afraid to be vulnerable. Instead of being afraid, take off the mask and free yourself from the barriers you've built around you; allow your true and authentic self to shine.

Be honest with your partner, because the number-one ingredient in any relationship is trust and honesty. If there is a lack of trust, then the relationship is in jeopardy. What's important to remember is that this goes both ways for you as well as your partner. When you trust each other, there is nothing to hide and you feel comfortable talking to each other about anything. Honesty is such an essential ingredient in healthy relationships, and so it is important to develop the habit of being open and honest about your feelings, or what's happening around you, without being afraid. However, be considerate and tactful when making a point. Whatever you do, don't yell, because that changes the energy in the room and affects your ability to communicate. Instead, speak with a pleasant tone of voice and use words of affirmation when necessary to help ease the tension.

Don't be too quick to interrupt or correct the other person; sometimes it's better to stop and think about whether or not it is necessary, or whether what you have to say will truly make a difference in the conversation. This can certainly help to prevent conflict in the relationship.

Many experts have stated that in order for relationships to grow and flourish, it's important to love and respect each other and to work together as a team. The Bible also tells us in 1 Peter 1:22 that we should "Love one another with a pure heart, fervently." I believe this means that you should not just express love verbally, but you should genuinely show love to one another by the things you say and do. Develop a sense of humour, but resist being pessimistic about the things you don't understand. Alternately, open your mind to new ideas and learn from them. In the end you will find that the possibilities are endless!

When you truly love someone, you love them for who they are, faults and all, and not for who or what you'd like them to become. Once you've decided to get married, don't try to change or fix your partner; instead, learn to accept the differences in each of you, because that's the same person you met before you got married. Now that you are together, learn how to live with each other's faults, and learn to compromise when things get a bit heated. Sometimes we find ourselves searching for the perfect person to make our lives complete. But what we tend to forget is that we all have faults, and that is what makes us who we truly are. Our life experiences are our own and should help us to grow in our own self-awareness.

I believe that God made us perfect in his own way, and he has empowered us to live according to his will and purpose to be all we need to be: loving, happy, and prosperous. But we as a people can never be satisfied. We try to change the things we do not like, the things we are afraid of, and the things we do not understand. In the end we become confused, and because of our selfish ways, we ruin it all. But if we can take a moment to accept our partners for who they are, and help them to realize the goodness within them, then maybe throughout this process they will eventually change the elements in their lives that are preventing them from being their authentic selves. And if we stop and take a good look at ourselves, we will also realize that we, too, need to make a paradigm shift and see ourselves for who we are. It's only then that we'll be able to do what is necessary so that we can be happy with ourselves. We will also realize that it is important to love ourselves before we make an attempt to love someone else.

Be kind to each other. Remember that life will test you all the time, so you can't allow the daily distractions to destroy what you have. When you speak to each other, speak softly and avoid harsh words. When you find that things are becoming too much for you to handle, don't allow yourself to get caught up in a fight, which will cause you to lose sight of what's right and what's wrong, and you will not be able to think clearly or make rational decisions. Walk away from a quarrel and return when you are calm and ready for a conversation. Think of it this way: when you are driving in the midst of a storm: you become so overwhelmed that you can't see clearly to figure out which way to go. Eventually, you have to pull over and wait for the weather to calm down in order to proceed.

Life's about choices, and the choices we make in our relationships can certainly affect our lives and change who we are. We are what we think, and our thought processes also affect our lives in a very big way. Therefore, it makes sense to avoid thoughts that are mean and hurtful. Instead, think positively about others and the situations in your relationships. Show interest in each other and celebrate birthdays, anniversaries, holidays, and all the special occasions in your life; this will help to show your partner how much you care. Be caring and considerate to each other, knowing that the good you do today will live long after you are gone.

Learn how to handle the strife in your relationships because this is a good sign of maturity. Many times when people feel hurt, their first instinct is to get mad or remain angry with the other person. If you find yourself in this situation, learn to forgive your partner, knowing that God forgives us daily for our sins and gives us second chances. The anger you feel will keep you stuck in that situation, but forgiveness helps to free your mind and allows you to move forward. Bryant Hill once said, "There is no love without forgiveness, and there is no forgiveness without love."

Throughout your relationship you will have disagreements, and you may have to apologize for your actions or words. If you are sincere, then your partner will most likely forgive you. When you are sincere about your love for each other, there will be no grudge, no competition, and no jealousy. You will learn to forgive and move beyond those things of the past, leaving yesterday behind and realizing that everything happens for a reason. Let's face it: sometimes there are things you just can't change. The love you have for each other should be love from the heart, a love that's pure and has no boundaries. When the love is real, it should help you to see beyond the simple things in life that can cause a disagreement or a quarrel, and then you can move forward with forgiveness. There is no doubt that as you move forward in your relationship, you will come to realize that you are responsible for the type of energy you create for yourself and the energy you bring to your relationship. You can choose to be happy by the things you do or say, realizing that the more effort you put into your relationship, the more you will gain from it in return. Set a good example for your children at home by loving and respecting each other. Do not argue in front of your children, because when you do that, it has a profound impact on their lives and change who they are. Showing respect to each other will help them to learn how to be respectful to you, their siblings, their friends, and ultimately their own partners when they grow up.

Throughout your relationships, don't expect others to fulfil your needs, complete you, or give you what you think might be missing, because this is not realistic and will never happen. What should be meaningful for you is the fact that you love yourself for who you are. Know that the love you truly desire is deep within you and that it's okay to allow that love to surface. Unless you are able to love yourself, you will not be capable of loving others.

Loving yourself means that you are sure of who you are, and you are satisfied. It also means that you understand your fears as well as your strengths and weaknesses and you are willing to accept them and move forward. In one of her shows on relationships, Oprah reminded us, "All life is energy and the world responds. You are responsible for the energy you create for yourself, and the energy you bring to others." Relationships are the most precious commodities anyone can have, but good relationships don't happen overnight. It takes time to get to know yourself and to experience that joy and love within, before you're able to share that love with others.

As your relationship grows, learn to be happy and appreciate the good in each other. One of the things you should be excited about is the fact that you both wake up together every morning to face a new day which holds for you unlimited possibilities. Take the time to thank God for life, health, love, prosperity, and each other. As you pray, ask God to teach you how to love unconditionally and give of your best to each other. Embrace your partner as often as possible and take the time to laugh together even at the simplest of things. In doing so, you will experience the magical effects of what laughter can do for the soul.

Nothing should prevent you from living a life that is authentic and full of love. Learn to evaluate your relationships. Don't do everything for everyone else and nothing for yourself. You have to learn to say no sometimes and offer a little bit of tough love once in a while. As long as you can be true to yourself, you will be able to express that joy and love by the way you treat others around you. Be gentle and kind, and extend a hand to your partner when he or she needs one to hold. Lend a listening ear when he or she needs someone to listen, and keep your shoulders steady when your partner needs one to lean on. The choices you make in your relationships are important and reflect the type of person you are. Choose wisely and be at peace with yourself, and you will build peaceful, loving, and lasting relationships.

Relationships with Your Children

Children are one of life's precious gifts. From the day they are conceived to the day they say, "I do," you will be responsible for them. Being a parent is an awesome experience which carries with it responsibilities. As a parent, you will be responsible for helping your child to develop physically, emotionally, morally, intellectually, and spiritually. Parenting is also about relationships with God and family. Don't be afraid to include God, other family members, and friends into your children's lives; sometimes it truly takes a whole village to raise a child. As they grow, instilling good values in them is of utmost importance. Teach your children to practice good habits because it will help them to develop good character. Proverbs 22:6 teaches us, "Train up a child in the way he should go: and when he is old, he will not depart from it."

As you care for your children and watch them grow, remember that each child is different with his or her own unique qualities, and each one should therefore be treated as an individual. Children need to feel safe so that they will always come to you without fear. It doesn't matter how young or old they are; children want to be seen and heard. They want to know that you believe that they matter and that you care. Children also like to feel respected, and they appreciate the fact that their parents or other adults take the time to listen to them and allow them to express themselves freely. Plan family time with them, where you'll be able to have discussions. Value their opinions even if you do not agree with what they have to say. This could be the perfect opportunity for you to have an open and honest discussion about a topic; you might be able to teach or guide them in different ways, and help them to look at the subject and analyze it. In the end they might even begin to see things from a different perspective.

Pay attention to your children and allow yourself to be present when they want to talk with you. In other words, stay in the moment and listen carefully. One way to show that you care is by turning off your telephone, the radio, and the television. Put aside anything else you might be doing and allow them to realize that they have your full attention. Children are very sensitive, so as they speak it is important to display a positive attitude. Do not interrupt or make annoying comments; this will give them the impression that you are not interested in what they have to say. Avoid any form of verbal combat and simply listen; this will help them to trust in you and to be open and honest with you. Teach them how to respect you and show respect to them in return; this will help them to realize that there are boundaries they are not allowed to cross. Just like your relationship with your partner, there should also be trust and honesty with your children. As you model this behaviour for them, they will develop the habit of being honest and trustworthy at home, at school, and with their friends.

Parenting is not easy, and there are no set step-by-step rules to follow that will work for every family or every child. Parenting as a whole is full of mystery and challenges, and you are bound to mess up sometimes. Occasionally you will even find that you are second-guessing yourself, but that is okay—this is all a part of life as a parent. You will make many mistakes along the way, and you have to be prepared for the countless number of questions your children will ask. Even if you don't have the answers for them, take the time to listen and allow them to ask their questions without fear. If you are able to listen and have a discussion, you might be surprised; maybe you will end up learning something new. Encourage their curiosity and love them for who they are. The fact that they are children does not mean that they don't have a voice and should not be heard. As you communicate with them, choose your words wisely. These words could be misinterpreted and ultimately end up causing them pain. When you say demeaning things to children, it makes them feel worthless and diminishes their self-esteem and their image of themselves. They might even end up holding that pain inside for a very long time because they are afraid to discuss their feelings. Eventually this could destroy your relationship with them.

As a parent, you are also their primary teacher and their role model. One of the best ways for parents to teach a child is by modelling good behaviour. Children often learn best by what they see, hear, and experience with the adults around them, so be careful of the example you set for them. They also understand that as parents, you play a very valuable role in their lives, and they will listen to you as long as you speak to them with love and respect. Teach them to be strong, to set goals for themselves, and to develop a plan of action in order to accomplish these goals. Teach them how to manage their time both at home and at school; this will help them to learn how to get things done on time without having to rush. Help them to understand that even though they are children, stress can take a toll on them and cause them to become sick. Therefore, it is important for them to get an adequate amount of sleep, eat healthy meals, and learn how to resolve the issues in their lives without being stressed. Teach your children to be kind. Allow them to be of service to others by volunteering with them at church or community events. Once they see you setting such a good example, they will learn that service to others is a good thing. This is very important because children will eventually grow up to become what they believe.

Teach your children to pray and to place God first in their lives. Teach them about love, and help them to understand that it is important for them to love themselves and show love to others as well. Teach them about courage, how to be brave in times of adversities, and how to be compassionate by being there for others in times of need. Teach them about honesty and integrity and the importance of being truthful at all times. Teach them about cooperation and taking responsibility for their actions. All of this should begin at home at a very young age. As a matter of fact, as a parent these are some of the behaviours you should model for them; this will allow them to learn how to trust you, follow your guidance, and live the lives you would want them to live. Love your children wholeheartedly and unconditionally. Affirm them every day by letting them know how proud you are of them and love them. Make them a priority in your life, and give them your undivided attention. Hug them, talk with them, provide for them the security they need, and create an atmosphere of trust, openness, and growth.

As your children grow, you will play different roles in their lives. You will be Mommy and Daddy, teaching them how to eat, sleep, walk, talk, dress, and remember the values you want to instil in them. As they get older, it is important to slowly learn how to give them the space and freedom they need to mature into the beautiful individuals they want to become. You should no longer want to do everything for them—or expect them to do everything exactly the way you would like. Allow them to look at life from their point of view, and be there for them when they fall. Forgive them for their mistakes and be sincere about it. Love them as your children, and if they ask for your help, do whatever you can in a positive way . . . and know when to let go. In the words of John W. Whitehead, "Children are the living messages we send to a time we will not see."

Create a loving and peaceful environment for your children. You don't have to snoop all the time, because you want them to know that you trust them. However, if you suspect that they are hiding things from you, and you believe that something is not right, then call them out on it. Don't forget to remind them that as their parents, you are responsible for them while they are home. It is also important for them to understand that you are still in charge and that you should be aware of whatever is going on in their lives at home and at school. Sometimes, as parents you will find that you'll have to administer a little bit of tough love, but that's okay; this is necessary at times because you want what's best for your children. No matter what happens, don't be submissive, and don't ever be afraid to let them know that as long as they are living in your home, they will have to abide by your rules. Explain that when the time comes and they become adults and are on their own, then they will earn all the rights they need to privacy.

As parents we tell our children to do the right thing, but most of the time we forget to explain to them what this means.

Once your children become teenagers, you'll find that you have your work cut out for you. Teach them that it's not okay to drink, smoke, or use drugs, and explain to them how dangerous this type of behaviour can become. Remind them that almost every day there are numerous stories in the news about children and young adults who drink or take drugs, and they either end up in serious accidents and die, or if they survive, they find that their lives have been changed forever. Point them in the right direction. Let them know that their lives are valuable and that if they feel pressured by their peers to get involved with drinking, smoking, or using drugs, then they should be strong enough to say no and walk away. These are some of the examples you can set for them at home. Once they see that you are not involved with drugs or alcohol, they will find it much easier to stand firm and develop the confidence they need to say no.

As they get older, teach them how to handle relationships, and don't be afraid to talk with them in very clear and concise ways about love, sex, and self-esteem. In order for this to be effective, there has to be an ongoing discussion. Help them to realize that it doesn't hurt to wait until they are old enough to understand and deal with the consequences of their actions in order to have sex. Explain to them that unprotected sex can result in pregnancy and that having a child at a very young age can change their lives forever. Teach them about the dangers of contracting sexually transmitted diseases, which can affect their overall health and sometimes be deadly.

Another important issue that is causing problems among teenagers today is the fact that they do not respect each other, and sometimes they fail to understand that when someone says no, that person means it. Teenagers need to understand that there are serious consequences, including jail time, if they are caught having sex with someone who is underage, or if the partner reports that he or she was raped. There are so many stories these days of teenage boys being accused of having sex with underage girls, and even though they claim it was consensual, they end up ruining their lives forever because the girls say otherwise. The same thing holds true for boys, so they also need to be careful. Teach your children how to ask for help when they believe they are in trouble, and encourage them to trust you. Make it very clear to them that they don't have to fit in with a group just to be popular, because being popular does not necessarily mean that people really like them.

Help your children to understand that it's important to choose their friends wisely. Learn how to speak with your teenagers openly about relationships. Don't be afraid to let them know that developing a relationship with someone they care about is a process and that there is no guarantee that they will end up with their first love for a lifetime. Explain to them that in relationships, break-ups do happen. If it should happen to them, even though it can be very painful, mentally, physically, and emotionally, it's important for them not to blame or punish themselves. Reassure them that they can always come to you and that you will love them and be there for them. Encourage them to love and take good care of themselves mentally, emotionally, and most of all, physically. Because if they feel good about the way they look, they will certainly feel better on the inside. Remind them that it's important to be happy, and take time to do the things they've always wanted to do. Life is difficult enough as it is, so you don't want them to feel as though they cannot have open and honest discussions with you about what's going on in their lives. In the end you'll find that these open discussions will help to dispel the myths and fears surrounding these very important issues. It will also help to give them the confidence they need to take control of their lives, look inside themselves, and find their inner light.

Teach your children to have faith, knowing that faith has no boundaries. Hebrews 11:1 states, "Now faith is the substance of things hoped for, the evidence of things not seen." Stay connected with your family and don't just sit with them for a few minutes each day. Instead, spend quality time with them. It's amazing how much time can be spent on the Internet, the cell phone, driving to and from work or school, or watching television. Don't allow the noise and other distractions around you to interfere with the quality time you need to spend together. Take time to break away from all of this and create the space to enjoy some peace and tranquillity with your loved ones. As a parent you also need quality time for yourself and your partner. Take time to relax and unwind from the everyday stress of life. As you spend quality time with each other, try to enjoy the things you like most. When you are able to de-stress, it will make you a happier and more loving parent and partner, and you will be able to build better relationships with your children.

Relationships with Children and Their Peers

There is no doubt that there is tremendous peer pressure on children today to be perfect or to do the things they would not normally do. This pressure can cause them to become overwhelmed, and they may find it difficult to develop friendships or to interact with their peers appropriately. Remind your children how important it is to choose good friends and to maintain lasting relationships. Every day they are bombarded with advertisements; they also have to deal with the added peer pressure at school. This bombardment makes life very difficult for them. Teach them about the power of self-control and delayed gratification, and how to handle these situations. Help them to understand that in life, one doesn't always get everything one wants. Teach them how to think positively about themselves, thus developing good self-esteem. Encourage them to stay healthy by exercising and getting enough sleep. As children interact with their peers, you will find that sometimes they hide things from their parents. Speak with them openly and honestly, and help them to realize that they can come to you and talk about whatever concerns they might have. Teach them to be honest, and remind them that even when things don't work out as planned, they should not get upset or become depressed. Help them to understand that disappointments in life can sometimes become a blessing.

Teach your children to love and respect each other, and to treat others the way they would like to be treated. In this age of bullying and so much confusion, there is an urgent need for you, as a parent, to sit down and have honest conversations with your children about the facts of life. You will also need to establish clear rules and boundaries. Allow time for open discussions with your children in order to increase their awareness about the effects of bullying in schools and on the Internet. Remind them that schools have codes of conduct, which are special rules for students to follow, and that you expect them to adhere to these rules. It might even be a good idea to sit with them and discuss these rules together; this will allow them to get a clearer understanding of what the rules are. As you have these discussions, they will also come to realize that you take these rules seriously. In this burgeoning age of social media, the boundaries of these rules are being tested daily by many students. Explain to them that sometimes students are not aware of the actions they perpetuate, or that there can be dire consequences and even legal implications for these actions. Therefore, it is important for them to be mindful of their behaviour in and out of school.

Children should be made aware that bullying takes many forms: physical, emotional, psychological, verbal, and sexual. Bullying can also take place by making mean, derogatory, defaming, and threatening comments to others or about them on the Internet and through cell phones. Sometimes these comments are written about teachers. As a parent it will be your responsibility to teach your children that this type of behaviour is inappropriate, hurtful, and unacceptable. Children should also be aware that being mean to those whose sexual orientation is different is a form of bullying. Have open discussions with your children about these topics. Teach them to respect each other regardless of their sexual orientation, their culture, or their disability; this will help them to develop healthy coping mechanisms, avoid self-destructive behaviours, and empower them to realize that they are not alone.

As your children develop these necessary skills, you will find that they are less likely to succumb to the amount of peer pressure around them, which could also lead to bullying. Have an ongoing dialogue with them so that they will understand the power structure in their peer groups. Discuss with them the consequences of their actions, whether or not they participate in an incident. Also, make it clear to them that it's important to speak up and not just stand by and watch from the sidelines without doing anything to stop the bullying. Let them know that they have a responsibility to thwart the bad behaviour of their peers, and to not aid or perpetuate their wrongdoings by yielding to enticements to bully others. By talking with them, you will have an incredible opportunity to teach your children right from wrong. These discussions will ultimately send the message of the way you expect them to behave with others around them.

Every child is different, but every family has to have specific rules or standards in the home to which children should adhere. Children should also understand that if these rules are broken, then there will be consequences. It is important to make sure that the consequences are connected to the behaviour so that there will be no misunderstanding. This does not mean that you have to incorporate corporal punishment. If they break the rules, talk with them first to get a better understanding of the reasons behind their actions or behaviours. Remind them once more about the rules, explaining that even though they may think that what they did was not a big deal, breaking the rules will not be tolerated.

Decide together as parents what the consequences should be for your children's bad behaviours. Even if there is no form of punishment at that particular moment, make sure they understand that what they did was unacceptable. It is important for children to clearly understand that there are consequences for their actions at home, in school, on the job when they start working, and throughout life in general. Be friendly with your children and have a good time with them; however, remember one thing: they are your kids, and it's important for them to realize that they are not your best friends. Once this is clear, you will find that there is respect at all times. Maya Angelou once said, "Insolent children and submissive parents are not the characters we want to admire and emulate."

In today's society, our children are living and learning in the school of life with friends from various backgrounds. With this in mind, the positive relationships you have at home with your children will empower them to go out and live a good life. Based on the values you've instilled in them, they will be able to build confidence and make good, informed decisions without being afraid. Even at an early age, you should take the time to be open and honest with your children; this approach will allow them to trust you as parents and to know that they are able to come to you for guidance as they get older, instead of listening to their peers. Help them to realize that there are people who are good and people who are bad; explain to them that there are people who will hurt them, even in their own neighbourhoods, and because of this, it is important for them to be aware of their surroundings at all times and never put their trust in people they do not know. Help them to understand how to spot those who are trying to con them into going to places with them, and how to handle these situations if they should arise.

We are also living in the age of technology where, with the touch of a finger, your child is able to access or send information globally. Technology has made the gap between parents and children much wider. Today more than ever, there are so many dangers lurking on the Internet, with people preying on young children. As parents it is pertinent that you monitor whatever your children are doing on their computers, tablets, cell phones, or other electronic gadgets. You should also be mindful of the music they listen to and what they watch on television, and do not encourage the use of drugs, foul language, or profanity. Take the time to share some of these moments with them as a family, whether it's by playing a game, watching a movie on television, or going to the movie theatre. Guide them as they grow, and teach them right from wrong when posting information on the Internet and social media with their peers. Interact with your children so that you can find out how they are doing and what they are thinking. Take the time to laugh with them, hug them, and tell them you love them daily, thus making them feel important in your life. Talk with your children about school, their friends, and the things they are interested in, and don't forget to praise them. When the time is right, reward them for their performance.

There are many of you who have not yet had the opportunity to experience the joy of parenthood, but I hope that one day you will. It is only then that you will be able to understand how precious children are in our lives. Each day I take time out to spend quality time with my grandchildren because they grow so quickly before our eyes. Once these precious moments are gone, we will never be able to recapture them. I will never forget the day my children came into this world; this was a very special time for us as well as our families. The first grandchildren of my in-laws; it meant a lot to me to see how happy they were. As the children grew up, we spent quality time with them, travelled on vacations, and had fun at parks. We did everything we could to protect them and gave them unconditional love. We were proud parents, and each child and grandchild allowed us to have such unique experiences. These are the memories that will live on forever.

Children begin their lives by being around their families, but as they get older and start school, they spend more time socializing with children their own age or a bit older. They tend to listen to their peers, and in most cases they want to be like them or would like to do the things they are doing. Therefore, it is important for parents to help them to form healthy relationships at a very young age. They will always have friends, and no matter what you do as a parent, they will be faced with pressure from their peers. Here are a few suggestions for you to help them deal with peer pressure:

- Spend some time around their friends and their parents.
- Take the time to get to know them, and teach your children how to promote positive friendships.
- Guide them and help them to develop confidence in themselves and build their self-esteem.
- Listen to your children carefully and value their opinions, because this will prevent them from having to seek advice from their peers.
- Teach them how to say no to their peers when they know that something is wrong.
- Encourage them to engage in after-school activities such as choir, football, soccer, baseball, or any sport which will help to boost their confidence. You will find that once they feel good about themselves, they will not succumb to peer pressure.

Although it is important for parents to have good relationships with their children, it is also important to understand that the relationships they develop with their peers are important. As they get older, it becomes more difficult for parents to pull kids apart. Yes, children are influenced by their peers, but most of the time the behaviour they display is based on what they've learned at home from their parents. As you raise your children, I encourage you to love them unconditionally, model good behaviour for them to follow, and be there to catch them when they fall. Don't forget that they are human beings and will make mistakes. Whenever they get out of line, remember that they are your children, and have honest and open discussions with them to get them back on track. Yes, they have to learn to take responsibility for their actions, but you also have to remember that all of this began at home, where you as the parent had the job of teaching them how to be responsible.

As parents, one of the deepest desires of our hearts is to see our children become successful, but sometimes things don't work out the way we would like them to. They will disappoint us, and some kids will give in to peer pressure. Whenever this happens, don't give up on them, because no matter what's happening, they will always be your children. Continue to build good relationships with them and be there for them when times get tough. Lend a hand when they need you the most, and don't forget that the day will come when things will change, and you will get older and have to live on your own. It's then that you will realize how much you miss them or need them in your lives, even if it's just to hear their voices in the next room.

In order to have a healthy and loving relationship,
it is important to be open and honest about money.

Lesson 7: Manage Your Finances

In today's economy, learning how to effectively manage finances can become a daunting task. The experts often say that one way to begin is to know how much money you have and what to do in order to keep track of how you are spending it. As human beings we are tempted to hide information from each other about our finances. But what is important for you to remember is that money is a very important part of your life, and the way you handle your money falls in line with the values on which you and your partner have decided to build your relationship. In order to have a healthy and loving relationship, it is important to be open and honest with your partner about money; you will find that it can be very difficult to meet your financial goals if you do not discuss this information.

Once you are together, it's no longer "my money" versus "your money", and it is not about who has the bigger paycheque at the end of the month. Your relationship should be about much more than that. You have decided to share your love, so why not share information about your finances, which will affect nearly everything you do? Set aside some time to sit down together and have this conversation so that you will have a better understanding of your partner's expectations about money. As you do so, lay everything on the table and figure out how to balance your expenses based on your income. It is true that we are conditioned to believe that men should make more money than women and that if we don't have money, we have nothing. But as important as money is, it should not be the reason you got together in the first place. Sit together, share your personal goals, support each other, and then plan for the future as a couple no matter who has the bigger paycheque.

Having a discussion about your finances is critical in order to have a wholesome and peaceful relationship; this type of discussion should be done with love and respect for each other. If you are open and honest about your financial affairs, it could be very helpful in determining who is more capable of handling the budget. However, this does not excuse the other party from his or her responsibilities. After all, this is a partnership, and it takes two to build a relationship. I would further suggest that once you've gone through the initial stages, where you've laid everything out in the open, you both should come to a decision as to who will be the main person handling the budget. Once this has been decided, make a plan to meet monthly and review everything. Consider this an important part of your everyday lifestyle and use the time wisely.

There is no perfect relationship whether or not one has money. But when two people live together, it is absolutely necessary that you learn how to share everything. You already share the physical space, the finances, and the household chores, so why not share your thoughts and feelings as well? As you discuss your finances, try to do so in a loving way. After all, this is one way of spending some time together and doing something that will have an impact on your lives. This will help to keep you both informed and help to prevent arguments. Find out what makes the other person happy and see what you can do to help. When it comes to your finances, this is not the easiest topic of discussion, but whatever you do, it should be done with honesty and integrity.

As you work together to manage your money, here are a few tips to help make things a bit easier.

- Take the time to be as organized as possible, ensuring that you keep good records.
- Know how much you both have, and then make a decision about how you would like to spend it.

- Set goals that are realistic; write them down, set realistic timelines, and save towards these goals.
- Develop a plan in order to make your money work for you. It doesn't matter if you are rich or just at a point where you can pay the bills.
- Develop a budget together. This is like a spending plan which will help you to meet your needs and to plan for the unexpected events or emergencies.
- Establish a savings account for yourself because this is one way of protecting yourself financially.
- Establish a joint account for emergencies pertaining to the household. Many financial experts say that it is important to have at least three months' rent or mortgage payment in your savings account for emergencies, such as job loss or illness, and there is no income from that person.
- Plan your spending in advance so that you both know exactly what you are working towards.
- Keep all your receipts in a special place and make notes of your spending so that your partner will be aware. This information will be very helpful when you sit down to review your spending and your budget.
- Balance your budget at least once each month, and pay your bills on time.
- Include an allowance for both of you in the budget.
- Save money for your retirement.
- Share information with your partner about outstanding debts, such as credit cards or other bills.
- Ensure that you have a plan where you will be able to monitor your credit reports to prevent and detect identity theft.
- Use your credit cards wisely, and do not go over the limit or accept more cards than you can afford to pay off.
- Develop a plan together for paying off your debts.

As you work together, you will find that throughout this process there will have to be some form of compromise in order to make things work. In the end, the important thing is that both of you stick to the plan. If your partner makes a mistake, don't be too quick to blame and to say things you will later regret. Don't forget that this is the person you love and that love does not give you the freedom to be mean-spirited or to magnify your partner's mistakes. Instead, take the time to talk about it peacefully and see what you can do to help. You may not even be aware of what your partner was going through at the time, so don't judge. Think about the situation, try to put yourself in your partner's shoes, and see how you would feel. If you judge without even knowing the reason behind the mistakes, it could cause a rift in the relationship. Know that no one is perfect, and you cannot allow your feelings to control your actions. It is better to be calm, understanding, and caring than to be critical and hurtful to each other. A loving conversation should be able to solve some of these problems as long as you work as a team. If you find that things are getting out of hand and too much for you to handle, it might not be a bad idea to seek help from a professional.

God has a purpose for your life, and no matter how hard you try to deviate from what is intended for you, it will eventually come to fruition. Therefore, it is up to you to find your purpose in life and work towards it. In all you do, don't allow the possession of money, power, and material things to cause you to stray from what God has planned for you. In order to have peace in your relationship, you have to be true to yourself and your partner. It is also of utmost importance that you live within your means and try not to spend more than your budget allows. As you plan your budget for your everyday life, try to save something for the future. One day you'll retire from your job, and it's only then that you will realize how much you need to survive.

Be true to yourself and purchase only what you need. More important, buy only what you can afford. So many times we buy on impulse or because we are stressed or depressed. Sometimes we go shopping because family or friends are going out to the mall, and we don't want to feel left out of that circle. Be strong enough to guard against these habits and find other ways to feel satisfied. If you feel depressed, go to the park and take a long walk. Listen to music which will uplift your spirit. If it's truly bad, get help from a doctor. If friends or family members are shopping and you feel you can't curb your impulse to shop, then don't go with them. If you happen to be the driver, drop them off at the mall and come to an agreement on the time and place for pick up; this will give you enough free time for yourself. You can go to the gym or do something else that you enjoy.

With all of the hustle and bustle at work, you owe it to yourself to make time in your busy schedule to be alone with your partner. Plan dates to be together, whether at home or on a trip to the beach, the movies, or dinner. It doesn't have to be anything fancy or expensive; the important thing is that your time with each other is enjoyable. You don't have to wait for everything around you to be perfect in order for you to be happy. If you truly want to be happy, don't allow your finances to get in the way. Make that decision to live one day at a time and enjoy life to the fullest; you never know what tomorrow will bring. Be considerate and understand that in order for your love to grow and stand the test of time, you will need to create space for each other to spend time alone and in private. We all need to take that moment to think, meditate, and recharge. As Kahlil Gibran once said, "For a love to grow through the tests of everyday living, one must respect that zone of privacy where one retires to relate to the inside instead of the outside."

Teach your children at an early age how to value and manage money appropriately.

Lesson 8: Teach Your Children about Money

As parents, you have many responsibilities. One that is at the top of the list—and that most people forget to do—is to teach children at an early age how to value and manage money appropriately. In doing so, it is important for you to be consistent and teach them in a way that is easy for them to understand. You should also be prepared to answer the many questions they will have. A good way to begin the process is by giving them a piggy bank as a gift when they are very young. Start teaching them how to save by using small coins and monetary gifts from friends and family. Encourage them to keep the money in their piggy bank until it is full. At this point it would be a good idea to sit with your children and teach them how to count the money and determine how much they were able to save. Don't be surprised if they become excited about purchasing a new toy or a new game; this is a great opportunity for you to teach them how to save for something special.

Once they've accumulated a certain amount of money, you might also consider taking them to the bank. Here they will be able to open an account which does not have service fees or special restrictions. While at the bank, the representative will be able to explain to your son or daughter the bank rules pertaining to this account. This experience will allow the child to hear from another person how important it is to value and manage money appropriately, and therefore they'll see things from a different perspective. The idea of having their own bank account can be an exciting experience for children, and the experience is one they will always remember.

I would take a step further and encourage you to monitor their accounts as they get older, to ensure that they are on the right track with their new financial responsibilities. Be aware of the daily advertisements which will surely get to them and their friends. Teach them to be patient because when they are patient, they will achieve more. Encourage them to wait until there is a sale on the item or until there's a special occasion before spending any money. This lesson will allow them to learn that it is important to plan for something they really need instead of shopping vicariously because they see it advertised on television or because their friends already bought it. Once they become teenagers, you will find that it is very difficult to convince them not to shop. This would be a good time to teach them how to invest their money so that they will realize that you really don't have to spend all the time.

There are too many young people who lack the necessary skills to handle money. Because of this, they are finding themselves in a lot of trouble and a mountain of debt. As your children get older, it is important to be honest with them about money.

- Teach them about the importance of making a budget.
- Teach them how to set aside funds in a savings account for emergencies.
- Sit with your children and explain to them how you have to make a budget in order to pay the bills and save for your retirement. You don't have to delve into all of the details, but provide enough information to make them realize that what you are teaching them is a necessary tool to prepare them for their future as an adult.
- Help them to understand that credit cards are not free money. In this era where plastic rules, they will get the impression that swiping a card is the way to go. Unfortunately, they do not understand the responsibilities that come with the card.

- Teach them how important it is for them to understand that just like their home, these banks have rules to which they will need to adhere.
- Impress upon them the fact that whether it's a credit card or a bank card, it does not come with unlimited funds. If they continue to spend more than they have, there will be consequences for overspending, such as having their account closed or their purchases denied at the cash register in the store.

This type of discussion will certainly help to open the door to personal growth. I remember hearing a great Chinese proverb: "Give a man a fish, and you feed him for a day. Teach him how to fish, and you feed him for a lifetime."

As parents you will find that the roles you play in the lives of your children are endless. While you teach them how to value and manage their money, you can also teach them how to become more responsible by allowing them to help out around the home. Many parents and children tend to believe that kids are entitled to an allowance as early as five years old. Today there are many debates about this among financial experts who believe (like I do) that this is not the way to go. When I was growing up, there was no such thing as an allowance; if we wanted extra money, we had to do extra chores around the house, or we helped out on the farm, where we were able to sell things to raise the extra money we needed. For us this was fun because not only did it give us the opportunity to do something different, but it also enabled us to learn about the concept of money and how to budget whatever funds we had. This experience also taught us how to think seriously about our wants and needs, and it forced us to prioritize our spending. Once we realized that we had to work for our money, there was no way we were going to use it all at once.

Having your children learn from a young age how to earn money by doing extra chores is one way of teaching them responsibility. This also helps to prepare them for the future.

If things are simply handed to children all the time, they will grow up expecting that this is the way of life and that it's not necessary for them to work hard for whatever their needs may be. The lessons you teach your children today about money are the lessons you hope will help to pave the way for a successful life in the future. These experiences are bound to live on in their memories for a lifetime.

Each of us has a special quality about us which makes us who we are. It sets us apart from everyone else and allows us to leave our mark on everything we touch. In caring for others, take the time to relax and also care for yourself.

Lesson 9: Take Care of Yourself and Your Family

Life itself is a journey, and in order to make this trip successful, you need to prepare for the unexpected and take care of yourself and your family. Each day take the time to eat healthy foods, including fruits and vegetables. Exercise daily if possible, and take the time to rest. As we watch television and read books and magazines, we are faced with a flood of information reminding us that it is extremely important to see the doctor. Don't just make an appointment when you are ill; prevention is the key to good health, so make it a habit to have a regular annual physical. If you see signs that something is not right with your health, don't brush it aside. You are not the expert on these things, so check it out. Even if you are a doctor, sometimes you need another opinion and someone else to care for you. You work hard every day, and even though at times you may feel invincible, don't fool yourself—you still need to take it easy and rest.

We are constantly bombarded by the media with "fitness experts" telling us which is the best way to stay in shape and lose weight, or trying to sell us their goods. They tell us daily that as few as ten minutes each day is all we need to exercise. Even though this is a great place to start, there is no such thing as "one size fits all" when it comes to losing weight or staying fit. I would suggest that you review what is out there and, along with your medical doctor, choose what is right for you and your needs. We all know that in order to stay fit and healthy, it's not the expensive machines or the personal trainer that does the trick. Instead, it's up to you. They are there to motivate and inspire you to make a difference in your life, but it's up to you to make the decision to change your mental outlook on life, stay on course, and do the work that is necessary. Educate yourself on how to lose the weight and work with it. Once you are able to do this, then the path to good health will be even more rewarding. As long as you believe in yourself and have the will to try, you will be able to achieve that goal. Whatever you do, don't make excuses—just go ahead and do it!

Learn how to eat well, and find a support group or someone you can trust to work with you. It's important to realize that it is still up to you to do what is necessary in order to lose the weight. As long as you are able to conceive it in your mind and believe that you can do it, then you will certainly be successful. Find a way to get rid of old habits that get in the way, and remain committed to doing the work. I'm not saying that you should give up all of life's little pleasures. A piece of chocolate, a slice of cake, a pizza, or even a scoop of ice cream or yogurt once a month to satisfy a short-term craving should not hurt. But for everyone it's different, so follow a plan that is best for you. Just like anything else in life, it is important to set a goal and work diligently towards it. In the end it's okay to reward yourself for being able to achieve that goal. Richard DeVos said, "The only thing that stands between a man and what he wants from life is often merely the will to try it and faith to believe that it is possible."

With all the hustle and bustle in life these days, work, school, and other activities take up much of our time, and fast food becomes the norm. Eating food that is good for your health should be one of your greatest pleasures. Just remember that without proper nutrition, your body and your brain will fail. Find foods that are easy to prepare, especially if you are busy or do not enjoy spending time in the kitchen. These days, everyone seems to be talking about going organic, and that can be a bit expensive. What you need to think about before you decide is whether or not you can afford that lifestyle. Try to eat as much fresh food, fruits, and vegetables as possible—whether it's from the organic food market or the farmer's market doesn't make a difference. There are many supermarkets these days with an organic section because they realize that more people are now concerned about their health. You will find that the fresh fruits and vegetables are good for you and will provide the vitamins you need. Food isn't just something that satisfies our hunger. As human beings, we use food as a way to comfort ourselves, to ease our pain, to learn about different cultures, to satisfy our cravings, or even to connect with others and develop new friendships. So whatever your plan is for your life, the bottom line is that you choose the food that not only will satisfy your cravings, but food that is healthy for you.

As you make plans to eat well, it may be a good idea to learn how to cook. You don't have to become a top-notch chef; you simply need to be ready to eat healthy and learn how to prepare your meals. It could be as simple as learning how to stir-fry vegetables or bake a chicken. If you find that you liked the way your parents cooked a certain meal, then instead of just thinking about it, ask for the recipe and learn how to prepare it yourself. In order to save time in the kitchen, plan your daily meals ahead of time; make a list of what you'll need and what you will need to purchase at the supermarket or the farmer's market. When it's time to prepare the meal, organization is the key. If you do not like to spend a long time in the kitchen, you can do what I've been doing for years. Cut down on preparation time by cleaning, washing, chopping, and preparing your vegetables and seasonings before you are ready to start cooking. The vegetables can be placed in the freezer or the refrigerator, where they will remain fresh. Having a good meal on the table is one way to bring the family together. Once you've learnt to cook, why not show off some of your culinary skills and invite friends and other family members to join you?

Establish mealtime in your homes so that you can spend time eating together as a family. Mealtime is about family time; it's about love and it's an opportunity to connect with each other. Even if you are living alone, it's a good idea to establish personal mealtimes and stick to it. Eating together helps you to develop a close family bond. When I was growing up, this was a ritual in our home, and today I continue that tradition with my children and grandchildren. Before each meal we pray together, thanking God for all that we have and asking him for blessings on those who helped to make our meals possible. As you sit down to eat, you are not only sharing a meal, but you are also sharing each other's company. This is also a good time to share your stories and ideas, to talk about school, work, your culture and family history, or life in general. But most of all, you will be spending quality time together. This type of interaction will help the children to learn about their cultural heritage and get a better understanding of why you choose to live the way you do. You will also find that having these discussions will help to make your children feel more comfortable expressing themselves, because they know that this is a safe place to be open and honest. I believe wholeheartedly that a family that prays together and eats together will stay together.

In everything you do, always aim to set a good example for your children.

- Pray daily and give God thanks for your family and all that you have.
- Develop good work habits and go to work on time. You will find that your day will begin and end with less stress.
- Learn how to work with others as a team.
- Take pride in your work and do your share of the job well.
- Each day, pay attention and try to learn something new in order to make the work more meaningful.

In this age of technology where everything is changing on the job, it behoves you to stay current and know what is going on in your organization. It is also important to look ahead and participate in various forms of training so that you don't get stuck in a rut. You never know when a new position might become available, and because you have the training, you might just be the person they consider for this job.

Whatever path your life's journey should take, it is imperative that you maintain your credibility with others around you by doing the things you say you are going to do. Don't allow doubts about your ability to form huge barriers in your life; they will limit you and prevent you from accomplishing whatever you set out to do. Be careful with whom you align yourself, whether as friends or co-workers. This is important because sometimes you will find yourself in positions where your job may require that you exercise a certain amount of discretion in what you are able to do or say to others. Sometimes you will find that co-workers can become pushy and persistent, so be on guard. There are times when you will come across people who are arrogant and behave as though they know it all. In most instances these are the people who have made many mistakes previously, and therefore they are not the people you'll want to listen to for advice. If you want to be successful at what you're doing, you should be willing to make the changes that are necessary in your life. Here are a few tips to help you become more successful on the job.

- Keep your word, and people will respect you for that.
- Tell the truth at all times, and choose your words carefully.
- Choose your friends wisely, and be careful how you deal with the people around you.
- Learn to be humble.
- Learn how to adapt to changes, and be flexible and willing to go the extra mile.
- Look at things differently, and learn new ways of doing things.
- Learn to think on your feet, and be proactive.
- Avoid getting caught up in the noise and confusion of others on the job and those around you, because this can become extremely stressful.

Manage the Stress in Your Life

Uncertainty can cause anxiety, but you have to learn to train your mind to relax. Today more than ever, more people are suffering from stress-related issues, and doctors have made it clear that stress is a silent killer. How you manage the stress in your life will be very important if you wish to remain healthy and alive. Be realistic and handle things appropriately and on time. Don't fool yourself into thinking that you can operate best under pressure. We all know that it does not make sense to leave important things for the last minute, and then you have to rush to finish in one day what you should have done over a week. You will find that the work you do will be mediocre, and you will always be second-guessing yourself. If you operate this way, you are certainly setting yourself up for failure. Whether you are going to a job or a doctor's appointment, or whether you're going out with family or friends, try to be on time. It might not be a bad idea to leave at least ten minutes early, especially if you know you might encounter traffic. Whenever you have to rush, it takes a toll on your body, and you will find that once you arrive at your destination, it takes a longer time for you to settle in and get comfortable. Most of all, the people who are waiting on you will find this habit of lateness to be very disrespectful.

We are all faced with stressful situations every day, and most of the time it's because of what we do. It is essential for you to identify the stressors in your life and learn how to deal with them or get rid of them. If the stress becomes too much for you to handle on your own, seek help from family members, co-workers, friends, or a professional. How you handle the stress and the noise around you is crucial to your overall health. If the stress is caused by too many tasks on the job or by too many things to work on at home, learn how to let go and delegate. This extra pressure on you might even be a result of family or friends or co-workers around you; if this is the case, learn to avoid those who are difficult to deal with, and don't allow them to involve you in their drama. If the extra stress is connected to your social life, take time to re-evaluate your schedule and slow down a bit. Whether or not you are married, relationships can be stressful, and stress can also put a strain on your relationship. Take the time to evaluate the situation, weigh your options, and eliminate whatever unnecessary activities and commitments might be weighing you down.

Stress can affect your blood pressure; cause depression, insomnia, and terrible headaches; and increase heart rate and be harmful to the heart. It can weaken the immune system and make one vulnerable to other illnesses. Learn to relax and get things done on time, and stop worrying about the things you cannot change. Whenever you find that you are stressed, pay careful attention to your diet. At times like these, some people tend to eat too much, eat the wrong type of food, or eat nothing at all. None of this is good for your health and can cause things to get out of hand. Make good choices for your daily life; choose to eat healthy foods because they will make you feel more alert. Take long walks so that you can feel free to think clearly and find a balance between work and time for yourself.

As you work on eliminating stress in your life, it's important to get organized. You will find that if your surroundings are disorganized, it creates added pressure. Take the time to clear out some of the clutter around you each day, especially in your work area; this will certainly help to make you feel much better. Create time in your daily schedule to exercise and learn how to breathe properly. Meditate as often as possible in silence; this will help to keep both your mind and body in shape. For the ultimate bonus, treat yourself to a massage every now and then. You will find that this will not only help to relieve the stress and your aches and pains, but it will help to improve circulation, improve your emotional well-being, and relax the whole body. Make every effort to sit down, relax, and eat a healthy meal. You will find that by exercising and eating healthy, your body will regain the strength you need to live a full and stress-free life.

As you pay attention to your outer body, it is important to care for your inner body as well. Be careful what you feed your mind through the information you let in. Don't try to handle all that life throws at you at once; learn to take things one step at a time. Don't worry about the past or the future; simply live as much as you can in the moment, focus only on what you are doing right now, and enjoy it. Stay positive and try not to worry about the things that are insignificant, that you cannot change, or that you can't control. Set certain standards to live by and do not compromise your values. Manage your stress by changing the way you look at things. When you do this, you will find that your whole outlook on life will be different.

In all that you do, don't forget that God loves you and allows you to be surrounded by your family, friends, and all that you have. In order to feel the love from others and to feel truly fulfilled, it is necessary for you to have a loving relationship with God. If you allow God to be first in your life, then the relationships with your family will be loving ones. Once you are able to put God first in your life, not only will you be happy, but you will find that you'll become a more balanced and productive person. Each of us has a special quality about us that makes us who we are; it sets us apart from everyone else and allows us to leave our mark on everything we touch. In caring for others, take the time to relax and to care for yourself. Take some time to examine your life to see how well you've been living. Learn how to make good choices and understand that there are consequences to your actions. It does your body no good if you are going to work yourself to a frazzle. Life is a precious gift, so don't waste it, because later on you will find that you end up regretting the things you've done that you will never be able to change or take back. Instead, take time for yourself to rest and recharge. Maya Angelou said, "Since life is our most precious gift and since it is given to us to live it but once, let us so live that we will not regret years of uselessness and inertia."

In all that you do, put God first in your heart and make him the centre of your life. Everything else will fall into place.

Lesson 10: Nurture Your Spirituality

As you continue on your journey through life, don't forget that you are a spiritual being and that the material things in life are not enough to make you feel fulfilled. In all that you do, put God first in your heart and make him the centre of your life. You will find that everything else will fall into place. In order for this to happen you will need to create that space and time to focus on his words and grow spiritually with him. Spend this quiet time daily and realize that your faith in God is renewed and that you will become more spiritually centred. When times get tough, you will hold on to your faith to develop a reservoir of strength and divine hope to pull you through them. I believe that God has more in store for you than you can ever imagine. Therefore, do not limit yourself to the small things in life. Think big, take that bold step, and move forward with confidence, fearing no one and nothing. Know that whatever you desire in life, you can have it because you truly deserve it.

God has a plan for all our lives and will always be there for you if you believe in yourself. If one day that big break you were hoping for does not materialize, and you suddenly become disappointed and want to give up, just remember that sometimes God uses disappointments to steer us in the right direction and get us to where we need to be. We could say that this is a part of his divine plan for our lives. Don't be afraid and sit around in self pity. Get up and shake the dust off your feet. Take on a new attitude, bolster your confidence, and move forward. As you read the Bible, you will realize that God's grace is sufficient and forever present.

Everyone wants to be happy and successful, but it is important to remember that happiness is a by-product of success.

In order to be successful and nurture your spirituality, you have to make a decision about your purpose in life. You need to have a plan and work towards that purpose. You can focus on improving your skills by attending classes. You can also volunteer and be of service to others while doing something you enjoy. Learn how to become Christ-centred. Turn to God through prayer for strength and believe that he will grant your wishes. Each day give thanks for what you have and develop a good relationship with your family and others around you. This is one way of achieving the happiness you are looking for and that you deserve. Ultimately, true happiness lies within you; all you have to do is believe in yourself and take the time to experience it. Belief in yourself can help you to eliminate worries and anxieties, and it can cause you to experience a sense of calm and peace inside. It can give you a renewed spirit and guide you to make the right decisions. The great leader Mahatma Gandhi once said, "Happiness is when what you think, what you say, and what you do are in harmony."

We all have things we have gone through in life that we feel we can never forget. But don't allow the stress and emotional conflicts to hold you down, because they will destroy your health and your spirit. Instead, think of it as a part of life, as things you had no control over, and do what is necessary to move on. Don't try to fight battles that are not important enough to make a difference in your life. Learn to put the past behind you and focus on the present. Whenever you are faced with adversities in life, don't ever give up. Develop a fighting spirit and stay on course, believing that God has your back and will pull you through. Each day as you wake up, give God thanks for a new day and for life. Ask him for wisdom and protection as you move forward to do the things you have planned. Invite God into your life daily and acknowledge him in everything you do, and he will clear the way for you. He will open new doors to success. He will even work miracles for you. The things you never expected to happen will come to pass.

Being positive can be difficult sometimes, and yet it is so important. Thinking positive thoughts daily will empower you to see things from a more positive perspective, and in the end you will be able to live a life that is fulfilled. I find it inspirational to read good books, read the Bible, and listen to inspirational music daily; this approach helps me to stay calm and meditate peacefully. My friends sometime say to me, "With all that is happening around you, how do you manage to stay so calm?" I smile because I know who I am, and I'm certain that what I'm doing is working for me because of my faith in God.

Whenever you're feeling down and everything you try to do seem hopeless, take the time to listen to the teachings of people who are inspirational. These are people who will motivate you to do what is necessary to fulfil God's purpose for your life and live your best life each day. Some of the great spiritual leaders, such as Dr. Deepak Chopra and Dr. Wayne Dyer, tell us that spirituality requires practice and that spirituality is the essence of everything. They encourage us to practice to be still for a period of time, to breathe and bring peace into our lives and space, and to listen to that voice within. I encourage you to take the time to do just that. Do not get caught up in the daily rush of things. Be calm and take things slowly, one moment at a time, so that you can hear God's words and can look at success from a spiritual perspective.

Listening to good music can also help you to stay positive. I am reminded of Jamaica's legendary reggae artiste, the late, great Bob Marley, who inspired people around the world with his music. No matter which country you visit, if you listen keenly you will hear his music playing either in a restaurant, a bar, or a nightclub. I was surprised to hear his music in a restaurant in the Netherlands as my friend and I sat down to have dinner. The people in the restaurant were very calm as they enjoyed their meal and listened to the music. We couldn't help but listen carefully to the lyrics of the songs, because they were so inspirational. It's not like I'd never heard these songs before—it was just that I'd always been too busy to sit down and really listen to the words of the song. One that stood out for me is titled "Positive Vibrations". In this song Bob Marley encourages us not to fuss or fight, but to help each other along the way and make it a positive day. We both found these words to be very powerful, and this helped us to start a wonderful conversation.

As you work on your spirituality, it is important to learn how to resolve the conflicts in your lives. If someone says things to you that are too painful for you to hear, don't be bitter. You must take time to separate what is truth from what is unreal. Learn to forgive and release that person from all the confusion so that he or she will be able to experience the goodness of God. Forgive your family and friends who've hurt you in the past, and you will free yourself from all the pain and anger. The anger is just an outward manifestation of all the hurt you are feeling inside. If your relationship ends, don't harbour hate because it only makes you feel weak and defeated. Holding on to the anger will not help to restore what you've just lost; instead it will make you bitter, and you will never be able to move on and develop new relationships. However, be careful of the choices you make as you move on with your life and connect with people who are worthy of your love and your time. As Bishop T. D. Jakes said, "Because the flower has bloomed and withered away does not mean you must plant a weed just to have something in its place."

Forgiveness is a part of the healing process, which allows you to focus on what is ahead, grow in faith, and move forward. If you keep the anger inside and dwell on the negative, then the anger will burn a deep hole inside your soul and draw more negativity into your life. If you dwell on the past, the pain will return and keep you from reaching that peace of mind you so deserve. But when you learn to let go of past hurts and forgive yourself and others, you reduce your anxiety and all internal conflicts. As you learn to forgive, God will bless you, and you will become stronger. You'll open new doors in order to experience a deep connection with your spiritual being. Life is precious, and connecting with your spiritual self is truly the beginning of self-awareness.

God has a great plan for your life, and he will create new opportunities for you if you remain faithful and hopeful. Maintain a good balance in your life and reach out to help others in need. A little kindness goes a long way and will make you feel good about yourself. The choices you make in life are important, and when you do something to help others, you will achieve spiritual fulfilment, because as you help others, you are also doing something that will help to uplift your spirit. Acts of kindness don't normally go unnoticed. Before you know it, they can create a chain reaction with infinite possibilities. Choose to be with people who are positive and who can help lift you up and help you be all that you want to be. Learn to be humble; don't be selfish and think about yourself. Instead, be kind to others, allow your instinct to guide you, and live an exemplary life so that others might learn from you.

Because the world we live in is extraordinarily diverse, respecting people of different cultures is a very significant task. Learning about the different cultures can be extremely helpful in breaking the cycle of racial barriers and prejudices.

Lesson 11: Be Culturally Sensitive

Our classrooms and workplaces are becoming more demographically diverse. Many of you will travel to different states or different countries to visit, study at universities, or work in various organizations. Learning and working in a culturally diverse or multicultural environment requires that you have a conceptual understanding of the different cultures and a respect for the integrity of different cultural perspectives. As you assimilate into your new environment, it can be very easy to get caught up into what is happening around you. Whatever you do, remember not to abandon your culture. Through this process of assimilation, you will learn the customs and norms of this new community; sometimes you will even have to learn the language so that you will be able to work, learn, and live comfortably in that community. You will learn to make some adjustments to your normal way of thinking in order to fit in and become more culturally sensitive.

The issue of cultural sensitivity does not exist only in schools and our work environments; it also exists in the environment in which you will live with people of diverse cultural backgrounds. Therefore, it will become necessary for you to learn as much as you can about the different cultures, and to develop cross-cultural communication skills. This will help you to value and appreciate the differences and similarities not only among people of different cultures but among people with different sexual orientations, people with disabilities, and people whose lifestyles, work habits, and study habits are different from yours. Understand also that it is good to be able to question other people's ideas without being disrespectful; this is how you will be able to learn from others as well as share information about your cultural background and your rich heritage.

Encourage others to ask questions, and be willing to answer in a way that they will be able to learn something new about your culture. If you are able to understand the values and beliefs of others, then you might be able to see how this influences their behaviours. Be mindful of the words you use to describe someone or a group of people. Words that are inappropriate can reflect ignorance and a negative attitude towards others. People around you might even find these words to be offensive. Instead, use words that are more acceptable and respectful so that you will be able to build good relationships. In your new cultural environment, you are bound to experience "culture shock" due to the extraordinary mix of cultures and unfamiliar lifestyles, but it is important to understand that this happens to all people when they move to a new community or a new country. As long as you learn how to develop good relationships with others, you will do just fine.

I remember when I first moved to Florida and started teaching at a high school; I was greeted by students from different cultural and socioeconomic backgrounds. For me this experience was nothing new because I had lived in New York, one of the most multicultural environments, for more than twenty-five years. One morning I wore a pair of earrings and a bracelet with the colours black, green, and gold. I did not think much of it because they were very small and it was not against the rules. I did not care to wear any expensive jewellery to attract unwanted attention. It was amazing how these earrings and bracelet helped to spark conversations with both students and teachers. They wanted to know more about me and why I was wearing those colours. According to them I did not have what they considered to be a Jamaican accent. This exchange afforded me the opportunity to tell them a little bit about my country and my cultural background. For many of them, this was something new; everything they knew about Jamaica was based on what they heard in songs on the radio, what they saw on television, or what they assumed based on their brief encounter with Jamaicans in their communities. It was quite obvious that they never took the time to ask questions and that no one took the time to explain anything to them.

Because of this interaction, the students' assignment was changed: it was now time to get to know each other a little better. Students began to share information with each other about their cultural backgrounds. Many were surprised to learn about the differences and similarities among them. I believe this time they spent sharing helped them to develop a better sense of appreciation for their own cultures as well as that of others in the classroom. These discussions were described by many students as one of the best lessons they'd ever learned; this became evident later on in the way they treated each other and the respect they began to show each other in the classroom. Because the world we live in is extraordinarily diverse, respecting people of different cultures is a very significant task. Learning about the different cultures can be extremely helpful in breaking the cycle of racial barriers and prejudices.

Adjusting in this environment can become a daunting task for children, especially when they enter a new school without their friends and are not prepared for this change. They might feel intimidated by others because there is so much to learn and they are not sure what to expect. Bear in mind that this is also difficult for those children who have already settled into the school, because they will have to learn how to deal with these new students. As a parent you can help to provide a smooth transition by spending time with your children as they settle in and helping them to learn about the different cultures and customs. As they adjust to their new environment, teach them how to make new friends and how to respect others even if they are different. The way in which children relate to others will certainly have an impact on their relationships with them.

Teach your children that if someone is new to their community, speaks a different language, or has a distinct accent, it is certainly not a good reason to dismiss the person. Help them to understand that good communication is vital for building relationships, and this might be a great time for them to learn a new language and establish new friendships. Conversely, it is important for your children to be tolerant and realize that newcomers may not understand *them,* either. Help your children to realize that if they are willing to change some of their behaviours and attitudes, they will certainly see an improvement in their relationships with others. Teaching them about the importance of tolerance, respect for diversity, and inter-cultural dialogue will help them to feel more closely interconnected. Kofi Annan, a former secretary general of the United Nations, said, "Tolerance, inter-cultural dialogue, and respect for diversity are more essential than ever in a world where people are becoming more and more closely interconnected."

As parents you are responsible for setting a good example for your children. Be aware that your beliefs can be reflected in your speech and your behaviour towards others. As you settle in, challenge yourself to make a positive difference in everything you do. Remember that we are all different and that people are blessed with multiple talents which can be used to solve complex problems. This is critical, because whether you are in school or on the job, you may be required to work on projects as a team. One way to prevent conflict is by valuing the differences in opinions, ideas, experiences, abilities, and ways of learning, and by showing respect for the beliefs of others.

Learn to accept and embrace the beauty and spirit of other people around you, and embrace their culture and their religion. You might be surprised at how much you will learn from each other and how beautiful a relationship you'll be able to develop. You will also find that it is much easier to live together in harmony than to be completely miserable and unhappy in your own community. Don't get angry the minute you hear someone saying bad things about you, your ethnicity, or your culture. Do your best to remain calm and take time to think, remembering that your thoughts and words create your reality. Once you are able to allow that emotion to marinate within your heart, you will be able to react or respond from a more conscious point of view. No matter what happens, you should not allow the negative emotions to break your spirit. In life you have but one shot to be happy, so live today as if it is your last and don't dwell on the past mistakes, whether yours or others'. Instead, find happiness in whatever you are doing with the people in your life, and move forward with love in your heart and faith in God. Simply live, laugh, and love!

Finally, set the standards by which you wish to live, and don't allow anyone to use you, abuse you, or walk all over you. As you speak with others, listen carefully to what they have to say and respond to what is being said, instead of reacting to *how* it is said. When conflicts arise, it is best to evaluate the situation by asking questions and avoiding certain facial expressions such as anger, shock, or amusement, because these are signs of bias which could lead to confrontation. It was Sir Isaac Newton who stated, "For every action, there is an equal and opposite reaction." Treat people as individuals and not based on your perceptions about them. Think about the biblical rule, which encourages us to do unto others as we would have them do unto us. You only have one life to live, so why not live your best life now?

One of the things I've experienced as a mentor is that my happiness comes from doing things for others. Having the opportunity to realize that I've made a difference is the extra bonus!

Lesson 12: Become a Mentor

Behind every successful person, you will always find someone who took the time to care. Mentors are people whose primary goal is to help their mentees, who are less experienced with their personal and professional development. Throughout the mentoring process, your mentees will be given the tools or resources needed to master new skills and gain additional knowledge. There are many organizations with mentoring programmes, and it's a good idea to connect with one. However, you can choose to become a mentor on your own. This can be done either through a school, through a church, or while on the job. Whatever you decide, it is important to realize that mentoring is a partnership and that both parties can benefit tremendously from this valuable relationship.

Some people think that mentoring is difficult and time-consuming, but there are many others who enjoy being a mentor. You would be surprised to see how much of a difference you can make in someone else's life if you spend a little time with them. Mentors are people who truly care about others and are willing to share their time, experience, and expertise in order to help them move in the right direction. As a mentor, your main focus is to help those you are mentoring make a decision about what their goals are, and you also help them to develop action plans in order to achieve these goals. Even though you may not be working in the same environment or attending the same school, you can be a positive influence and provide a different perspective on things. You may also be able to help your mentees solve a problem or make a decision that will profoundly affect their careers or their lives in general. Doing big deeds is awesome, but sometimes it's the little things you do that make the difference in someone's life.

Once you've decided to become a mentor, it is important to remember that people are different and that your personalities may not be the same. Be prepared to answer many questions, and when you are not sure about something, don't be afraid to say, "I don't know, but I will look into it." You will find that your mentee will respect you for that and will realize that you are not perfect. As you interact with your mentee, be as authentic as possible and model positive behaviour. Build good relationships with your mentees and allow them to realize that they do not have to face their struggles alone. While you work with them, take your time, be patient, and don't expect them to know everything—if they did, then there would be no need for you to be their mentor!

I've been a mentor for over twenty years, and I've been fortunate to be in a position to mentor students as well as co-workers. Even though many of them have moved on to various organizations, tertiary institutions, or have graduated, we still keep in touch. I've found mentoring to be a very rewarding experience, and it has encouraged me to want to do more for students of all ages. One of the things I've experienced as a mentor is that my happiness comes from doing things for others. Having the opportunity to realize that I've made a difference is the extra bonus! I have also come to realize that what I truly desire is realized through the paradoxical means of desiring the same thing for them. Whatever I'm able to share with my mentees returns to me in many ways.

Mentoring is truly a volunteer position for someone who cares and is willing to remain committed to this task. As a mentor you will work with your mentees to build trust, to inspire, to encourage, to motivate, to teach, and to impart new and different ideas or perspectives on things. But most of all you are there to listen to what they have to say. When you encourage others, you help to enhance their self-esteem and make them feel good about themselves. You help to lift their spirits and provide the extra boost they need to feel confident about what they are doing. You inspire them and give them hope to move forward. If you decide to take on the role of a mentor, here are a few tips for you.

- Mentor one person at a time, and develop a good relationship; this will allow you to remain focused on your mentee's needs and concerns.
- Have a casual conversation when you meet and find out as much as you can about the person.
- Ask about your mentee's background, and allow your mentee to share some stories with you about his or her life, culture, and family.
- Share your stories and experiences with your mentee; this will help to clear the air and make both of you more comfortable. This type of interaction will most definitely help you to develop a certain amount of trust and respect for each other.
- Work with your mentee to establish specific goals and objectives so that your time together will be well spent.
- Discuss a plan of action and set timelines to achieve these goals.
- Keep an open mind, take the time to listen carefully to what your mentee has to say, and try not to be the one doing most of the talking. Instead, provide feedback only when necessary.

It is important to understand that your mentees are there because they need help, and so they are the ones who need to express their feelings. Your job as a mentor is to listen, encourage, inspire, and motivate them to achieve their goals. In order to carry out your duties as a mentor, it is important for you to be reliable. Plan your schedule so that you are able to remain committed to a specific time period in which you will be available to meet with them.

While you work with your mentees, take the time to have fun and remember that being a mentor does not have to be a chore. Set a good example by being a good role model for them to follow. Be a source of encouragement, share your thoughts and ideas, and help them to identify the resources and connections that will help them to achieve their goals. Decide how long you will spend with one person, and when you are finished take time to celebrate and then move on to mentor someone else. However, it wouldn't hurt to stay in touch—who knows, you might be able to encourage that person to give back to others and become a mentor in the future! Go ahead and make that move, because in the end you will not only create exceptional experiences for others, but you will make a difference in someone's life. As you give back to others, know that you will become an extraordinary example to them, and you will be blessed abundantly.

Throughout the mentoring process, if you can help to light the path through someone's journey, then I believe that is what you were destined to do. Having a mentoring programme has helped me to connect people from the past with the present, thus creating opportunities for young adults whose lives have been changed forever. These mentors have not only been there to bring change to their mentees' circumstances, but in the midst of all this, they have found that it also brought a welcome change to their own lives. Mahatma Gandhi put it beautifully: "Be the change you want to see in the world."

In life we cannot expect to receive all the time—we have to learn to practice the art of giving. One of the things I know for sure is that there is an abundance of joy inside whenever I am able to do something I enjoy in life, while at the same time I'm able to give something or be of service to others. For example, whenever I speak with the students and others in my mentoring programme, and they tell me about their successes in school, on the job, or in their personal lives, it makes me feel happy knowing that I've had an opportunity to touch their lives in a small way. When you give from the heart or do something to help others, you are being of service to them, and it surely changes the way you feel about yourself.

One day the time will come when you'll be able to sit back and reminisce about your life. It's only then you will realize that the moments when you were truly happy were those times when you gave of yourself to others in a loving way. Suddenly you'll experience an abundance of joy inside, knowing that you've helped to make a difference in someone's life—you've actually helped to make someone happy. I know many people who are mentors and who've had mentors throughout school and their careers. They all agree that mentors affect our lives in some way. That special person continues to have an influence in our lives even when we get older. They've been there for us and have helped us to dream big dreams. In doing so, they've also guided us, inspired us, and most of all encouraged us to soar to great heights!

"You and I"

You and I,
we came together a long time ago.
Each of us from different worlds,
carrying with us our own thoughts, beliefs, and cultural norms.
When we met, we were merely strangers,
but today we've moulded our lives together
to create a relationship that is full of love, trust, respect,
and mutual understanding.
I admire your beauty, your strength, and your determination.
But most of all, I admire your extraordinary desire to make your
dreams a reality.
I appreciate the opportunity to learn about the different cultures
and to respect the differences and similarities among us.
I am thankful for the role you've allowed me to play in your life,
and I trust that God will grant me the strength to always be
there for you.
Today I make this promise to you:
I will be there for you in every way possible
for as long as I am able to do so.
I will respect you for who you are and the life you choose to live.
And as I remain with you on your life's journey,
I pray that God will grant you peace, joy, wisdom, and
understanding
to help you remain authentic in all that you do
and to live your life with a purpose!
As always, you have my love.

Your friend and mentor.

Conclusion

I see life as a huge classroom with many lessons to learn, experiences to share, and special friendships to forge along the way. We all have a role to play throughout each stage of life. I am very happy to be able to play my role and, in doing so, to touch the lives of so many young men and women. Mentoring others is my passion, and it makes me feel fulfilled. Each day I do all that I can to live a life that is very authentic, and I encourage my friends and family to do the same. I believe in quiet moments which allow me to think and meditate on the things that are important. I am also mindful of the things I do and the company I keep because I believe that spectators always see much better than those who are involved.

I pray that these life lessons that I've shared with you will place you in a position where you will take the time to stop, re-evaluate, reprogram, and re-channel your thinking about life. It is also my hope that what you have gleaned from these lessons of love will enable you to live your life much better today than you did yesterday. Tomorrow is promised to no one, and so it makes no sense to dwell on the mistakes of the past. Whether you are in the classroom or in the boardroom, you will need to be proactive and take responsibility for your actions. Take that leap of faith, choose to be the person God wants you to be, and understand that everything is in divine order.

Today more than ever, believe that you are destined to accomplish something extraordinary on your journey through life. Sometimes you will stumble or make mistakes, but remember that you are human and can't fix everything. Don't allow these small inconveniences to cause you to fall flat on your face. Know that everyone makes mistakes, and it's important to realize that there is a meaning behind each of them, a lesson to be learned. If you find that on your journey you get to a fork in the road and are not sure which way to go, think about all that you've learned along the way and choose the path of authenticity. This feeling of authenticity will allow you to be free to accept and enjoy the good things your life has to offer.

You are being asked to have a clear vision, develop good character, develop good leadership skills, be courageous, take care of yourself and your family, and develop your spirituality. Yes, this is a lot to aim for, but deep down you know that you can do it and that you are not expected to do this alone. Love your family and allow them to play a positive role in your life. You will find that they will love you in return and will be there for you. Lean on the word of God and have faith that he will see you through. Proverbs 3:5–6 assures us that God will be there to guide us in everything we do: "Trust in the Lord with all thine heart; and lean not unto thine own understanding. In all thy ways acknowledge him, and he shall direct thy paths." If you believe that this is possible and do what is necessary to achieve your goals, you will be successful.

On your journey you will meet many people from different cultures and different backgrounds. Along the way, take time to get to know a few by asking them to share their stories with you. As you have these conversations, you will get to know them better, probably develop new and exceptional friendships, and be able to find out what made them who they are today. Share your stories and your dreams with courage and conviction; you might just inspire them to develop the courage they need in order to do the things they thought they were not capable of doing. As you share your stories, you will get a better understanding of the different and unique talents you all possess, as well as those you have in common. John Maxwell stated it clearly when he said, "Having exceptional people on the journey with you, doesn't happen by accident. It's true that the greater your dream is, the greater the people who will be attracted to you."

Do not be afraid to dream big, but remember to wake up and take bold steps to make these dreams become reality. I do believe that in life there is nothing to fear and that too many of us go around worrying about the unknown. When you procrastinate, the fear becomes stronger and more overwhelming. Focus on reading the word of God daily and living on good principles, thus creating a balance in your lives; this will not only empower you to achieve your goals, but it will also allow you to become an example to others. I truly believe that when God is with you and you believe it, amazing things will happen in your life.

Whenever you are faced with adversity in life and things become chaotic, don't ever give up. You can't always expect everything to be easy. Charles "Tremendous" Jones once wrote, "Things don't go wrong to break your heart so you can be bitter and give up. They happen to break you down, and build you up so you can be all that you were intended to be." You will find that even though the road to success is paved with good intentions, there are many speed bumps, twists and turns, and sometimes huge potholes along the way. But with a little bit of courage, patience, and perseverance, I believe that you can ride slowly over the speed bumps, carefully navigate the twists and turns, and cross over the potholes without falling into them. If you think wisely, you will find a shortcut, an easier way to make it to your destination. Remember that it's *your* life, and your destiny is in your hands. I challenge you to take these life lessons seriously, make a paradigm shift, dig in your heels, and go for it! Always follow your dreams, and don't allow anyone to take them away from you. The journey towards achieving personal success and fulfilment in life starts with you!